In some ways the acid test for  infamous trial of Michael Servet Calvin's involvement in the tri: event seriously damages the integrity of the General reformer thought in their eyes. As Jonathan Moorhead capably shows, though, the case is much more complex. Moorhead's monograph is an extremely helpful study of a significant event of the French Reformation and reveals how the history of such difficult and intricate events should be written.

MICHAEL A. G. HAYKIN
Chair and professor of Church history, The Southern Baptist
Theological Seminary, Louisville, Kentucky

In convincing clarity Jonathan Moorhead takes us through all the facts of the Calvin *vs* Servetus case and comes to a precise and balanced conclusion. This conclusion finally does justice to the role John Calvin played in this indeed sad story. Moorhead's book confronts all those who for centuries have turned Servetus into an innocent martyr and a victim of Calvin's cruel rule in Geneva. Here we have the whole story and the true one, and thus a different one. The book reads like a good movie, but there is no happy end and there are no winners, except for the historical truth.

HERMAN SELDERHUIS
President, Theological University of Apeldoorn, Apeldoorn, Netherlands

There is an old saying, 'A text out of context is a pretext.' This is certainly validated in Moorhead's work, which focuses upon the infamous episode of the criminal actions of Geneva against Michael Servetus, the infamous sixteenth-century anti-trinitarian. This well researched study demonstrates the situation in Geneva and the Protestant Swiss cantons, forever exonerating John Calvin as the principal complainant and persecutor in the case. The book is a wonderful addition to our collective knowledge of both the times and of Calvin. I highly recommend it.

JOHN D. HANNAH
Distinguished Professor of Historical Theology & Research Professor
of Theological Studies, Dallas Theological Seminary, Dallas, Texas

John Calvin was the most influential theologian to the Reformation. His writings and ministry kindled the fire of biblical clarity and the structure of orthodoxy still accepted to this day. The one blight on Calvin's reputation that critics are quick to point out was his consent to the 1553 execution of Michael Servetus, a heretic who denied the Trinity, and therefore was tried and burned at the stake in Geneva. As with any historical event, Servetus' execution is riddled with complexities. Jonathan Moorhead sheds much-needed light on the events surrounding that infamous trial and execution. He demonstrates that Calvin's primary concern was not his execution, but his conversion. I strongly recommend this book to anyone interested in finding out what exactly transpired, and the broader implications.

JOHN MACARTHUR
Chancellor Emeritus, The Master's Seminary
Pastor-teacher, Grace Community Church, Sun Valley,
California

The Trial of the 16th Century is simply spell-binding! Once I started it, I literally could not put it down. Jonathan Moorhead writes in a fast-paced yet thorough style, bringing out key historical facts that not only help the reader grasp the vital background to the execution of Servetus in Geneva, but masterfully corrects some unfortunate erroneous suppositions about that sad event. As one who gives many Reformation tours in Geneva, I get frequent questions from visitors about John Calvin and the infamous Servetus incident. This book has become the key resource I suggest for those wanting an accurate understanding of the details surrounding that singular event in Geneva.

JOHN GLASS
Author of *A Walking Guide to John Calvin's Geneva*, and founder of
Calvin Tours Geneva (calvintours.com)

The TRIAL *of the* 16*th* CENTURY

Calvin *&* Servetus

Jonathan Moorhead

CHRISTIAN
FOCUS

Copyright © Jonathan Moorhead 2021

paperback ISBN 978-1-5271-0721-2
ebook ISBN 978-1-5271-0818-9

10 9 8 7 6 5 4 3 2 1

Published in 2021
by
Christian Focus Publications Ltd,
Geanies House, Fearn, Ross-shire,
IV20 1TW, United Kingdom.

www.christianfocus.com

Cover design by Daniel Van Straaten

Printed and bound by
Bell & Bain, Glasgow

CONTENTS

For my beloved Sharon

PREFACE

The execution of Michael Servetus (c. 1511–1553) is one of the most debated events in the life of John Calvin (1509–1564). It has left an indelible stain on his reputation and, unfortunately, the retelling of the story is often dependent on the historian's relationship to Calvinism.

Calvinists are prone to defend their champion while withholding less than flattering evidence. On the opposite end of the spectrum, there is a penchant for non-Calvinists to portray Calvin as an intolerant, murderous villain, which has led to myths that Calvin personally arrested, tried, judged and killed Servetus.[1] Even famed atheist Christopher Hitchens

---

1. For example, notice the title of William Drummond's book, *The Life of Michael Servetus: The Spanish Physician, Who for the Alleged Crime of Heresy, was Entrapped, Imprisoned, and Burned, by John Calvin the*

asserts, 'Calvin himself [was] a sadist and torturer and killer, who burned Servetus (one of the great thinkers and questioners of the day) while the man was still alive.'[2]

This dynamic produces an environment where one is hard-pressed to find an accurate account of what transpired. Did Calvin want Servetus to be executed? Did he try to lure him to Geneva to be killed? Was Calvin the Pope of Geneva that dictated the direction of the trial? Did he murder Servetus? What did irenic reformers such as Philip Melanchthon (1497–1560) and Martin Bucer (1491–1551) think should be done with Servetus?

It is the aim of this book to answer these questions and to give a faithful narrative of the role of John Calvin in the execution of Michael Servetus. For background, the life of Servetus will be examined with emphasis given to his education, publications, and relationship with John Calvin. His arrests, trials, and execution will then be discussed with attention given to the role of Calvin.

A significant contribution of this study will be to give more attention to cultural and political factors that were at play during Servetus' trial. Of interest for the twenty-first century reader is the context of executing heretics throughout history, and in particular, during the sixteenth century. The extent of Calvin's power in Geneva at the time of the trial is of critical importance, and little-known facts about Calvin's actions

---

Reformer in the City of Geneva, October 27, 1553 (Boston, MA: Little Brown & Company, 2008).

2. *God is Not Great* (New York: Hachette Book Group, 2007), 233. In perhaps one of the worst accounts of the burning of Servetus, *An Introduction to the History of Psychology* states, 'John Calvin ordered the famous anatomist Michael Servetus (1511–53) to be burned at the stake because he "described the Holy Land as a barren wilderness" (which it was), thus contradicting the scriptural description of it as a land of "milk and honey"' (B.R. Hergenhahn and Tracy B. Henley, Seventh edition [Belmont, CA: Wadsworth, 2014], 101).

during the trial will be brought to light. Reactions to the execution of Servetus during Calvin's life and beyond will then be shown in order to give perspective. Finally, the reader will be challenged to think critically about the ethics of telling history, the standards of properly judging previous generations, and the benefits of this study for the building up of the Body of Christ.

1

SERVETUS' EDUCATION AND PUBLICATIONS

Early Life

There is little information about the early life of Michael Servetus. This is unfortunate because it would be helpful to have a window into the development of his character and doctrine. What is known is that he was a native of the Spanish region of Aragon and was raised under the tutelage of Dominican friars.[1] By 1526 he was studying law in Toulouse, and through 1530–1531 he began to travel Europe. Notably, when he was around twenty years of age, he visited significant figures of the

---

1. Servetus' birthplace and birthdate are debated because of conflicting testimony by Servetus during his trials at Vienne and Geneva. For a helpful chronology of Servetus' life, see Roland H. Bainton, *Hunted Heretic: The Life and Death of Michael Servetus, 1511-1553* (Providence, RI: Blackstone Editions, 2005), 168–70.

Reformation: Johannes Œcolampadius (1482–1531) of Basel (even living with the reformer) and Martin Bucer of Strasbourg.[2]

Early on, Œcolampadius wrote to Bucer, Heinrich Bullinger (1504–75), Ulrich Zwingli (1484–1531), and Wolfgang Capito (1478–41) to warn them of Servetus' doctrine and belligerent attitude.[3] Even at this early stage in 1530, Zwingli admonished Œcolampadius: 'This is intolerable in the church of God; therefore strive in whatever way you can, not to allow his horrible blasphemies to spread abroad to the detriment of Christianity.'[4]

Following Œcolampadius' letter to Servetus which stated that his doctrine was of 'the highest blasphemy,' Servetus left Basel after ten months of being unable to convince Œcolampadius of his peculiar Christological views.[5]

Taking leave of Basel, Servetus then turned to Martin Bucer in Strasbourg, but was quickly asked to leave.[6] Servetus then brazenly returned to Basel, but the magistrates arrested him and ordered him to recant of his heresy.[7]

Servetus' distaste for the doctrine of the Trinity grew, and in 1531 he published *On the Errors of the Trinity* (*De Trinitatis*

---

2. Jeff Fisher, 'Housing a Heretic: Johannes Œcolampadius (1482–1531) and the "Pre-History" of the Servetus Affair,' *Reformation & Renaissance Review* 20:1 (2018), 35–50. See Jean Calvin, *Ioannis Calvini opera quae supersunt omnia* [= *CO*], 59 volumes, edited by Guilielmus Baum, August Eduard Cunitz, and Eduard Reuss (Bad Feilnbach: Schmidt Periodicals, 1990), 8:767.

3. *CO*, 8:744; cf. 8:866–68.

4. Quoted in Philip Schaff, *History of the Christian Church*, 8 volumes (Peabody, MA: Hendrickson Publishers), 8:715.

5. Ibid., 8:857. Œcolampadius evidences his understanding of Servetus' Christological views in his letter, 'To Servetus the Spaniard who denies that Christ is the consubstantial Son of God from Johannes Œcolampadius' (Bainton, *Hunted Heretic*, 33).

6. In a letter from 30 December 1531, Bucer assured Servetus that he would be safe in Strasbourg as long as he did not disturb or seduce anyone (*CO*, 8:868).

7. Bruce Gordon, *Calvin* (New Haven: Yale University Press, 2009), 219.

Erroribus, 1531) where he propounded views similar to the ancient heresy of Sabellianism (Modalism).[8] Denial of the Trinity would not be Servetus' only heresy: he also held to baptismal regeneration, rejected the doctrine of justification by faith alone,[9] believed that mortal sin was not applicable until the age of 20,[10] and rejected infant baptism (also condemned as heresy at the time).

The next year he wrote *Two Books of Dialogues on the Trinity* (*Dialogorum Duo*, 1532) where he retracted his theology, not on the basis of them being wrong, but because they were an immature representation of the truth.[11] Uncharacteristic of one who is now heralded as a model of tolerance, Servetus concluded his work by praying that God would 'destroy all tyrants of the Church.'[12]

Despite anti-Trinitarianism and Anabaptism being punishable by death according to the Imperial law of the Holy Roman Empire at that time, and the fact that heretics were executed in Basel and Strasbourg, it is important to note that Servetus was

---

8. Ibid. Sabellianism is the belief that there is one person in one God who manifests Himself in different ways. With this interpretation, Jesus is the Father. Contemporary proponents of this are 'Jesus Only' denominations such as Oneness Pentecostals. A notable figure in this movement is T.D. Jakes.

9. Schaff, 8:749.

10. See Michael Servetus, *Restoration of Christianity: An English Translation of Christianismi Restitutio*. Translated by Christopher Hoffman and Marian Hillar (Lewiston, NY: Edwin Mellen Press, 2007). At his trial, Servetus asserted that all sins prior to the age of 20 are not considered by God to be mortal (*CO*, 8:740.30–32).

11. In Michael Serveto, *The Two Treatises of Servetus on the Trinity* (trans. Earl Wilbur; Eugene, OR: Wipf & Stock, 2013), 188.

12. 'On the Righteousness of Christ's Kingdom,' *The Two Treatises of Servetus on the Trinity*, 264. As an example of this mischaracterization, Lawrence and Nancy Goldstone write that Servetus' 'crime was publishing a book that redefined Christianity in a more tolerant and inclusive way' (*Out of the Flames* [New York: Broadway Books, 2002], 1).

not executed in either city, but expelled.[13] Despite Œcolampa-dius' and Bucer's recognition of Servetus' heresies, the reason why Servetus was not arrested in these cities is likely due to the fact that he was a young man in his early twenties. Given that there is precedent for expulsion instead of execution, a valid question should be raised as to why Servetus was not expelled from Geneva. This will be discussed in Chapter 3.

Medical Training

As a result of the spread of Servetus' heretical writings, he changed his name to Miguel de Villenueva and lived for twenty years (1532–1553) hiding his true identity.[14] Servetus moved to France in 1534 and was active in Orléans, Avignon, and Lyons. In his travels he studied medicine at Paris and later at Montpellier. He wrote on controversial themes such as *Apology for Astrology* (1536), medical themes such as *The Universal Use of Syrups* (1537), and he edited Ptolemy's *Geography* in Latin.[15]

It is in Paris that we see early signs of Servetus' character that would be a significant factor in his Genevan trial. Namely, Servetus exhibited prideful behavior when the faculty of Paris censured him. Dean Thagault (Dean of the Medical Faculty)

---

13. On 11 August 1530, a month following the arrival of Servetus in Basel, Konrad in der Gassen was executed (beheaded and burned) for rejecting the New Testament, the power of prayer, the virgin birth, and Chalcedonian Christology. See S. Zijlstra, *Om de ware gemeente en de oude gronden: Geschiedenis van de dopersen in de Nederlanden 1531–1675* (Hilversun, Nederlands: Verloren, 2000), 75. See also Jeff Fisher, 'Housing a Heretic.'

14. Carter Lindberg, *The European Reformations* (Malden, MA: Blackwell Publishing, 1996), 269. Changing one's name for publication was not uncommon, and was even practiced by Calvin himself, who wrote under the pseudonym, 'Charles d'Espeville.'

15. Servetus refers to himself as a Doctor of Medicine from the University of Paris, but his graduation is debatable because of the faculty's disapproval of his views on astrology.

tried to persuade Servetus not to publish his controversial views on astrology, and recorded Servetus' response to this admonishment: 'He was abusive in the presence of several scholars and two or three doctors.'[16]

When Servetus persisted and published his *Apology for Astrology*, he was brought before a university council that was chaired by the president of the University of Paris, Pierre Lizet. When charges were brought against Servetus on 18 March 1538, the minutes record his response:

> The representative of the Faculty of Medicine complained that when the doctors remonstrated graciously Villeneuva had replied insolently. He had published not so much an apology as an invective against those who candidly admonished him. He, a student, accuses his teachers of imperiousness. He owes them respect as masters and instead he calls them monsters.[17]

Despite his negative disposition, Servetus is credited with the discovery of the lesser pulmonary circulation of the blood from the heart to the lungs.

Following his medical training, Servetus left Paris and practiced medicine in Lyon, Avignon, and Charlieu, France.[18] Significantly, from 1540–1553 he became the personal physician of his former Parisian classmate, Pierre Palmier (d. 1554), the Archbishop of Vienne, France.

---

16. Quoted in Bainton, *Hunted Heretic*, 75.

17. Ibid., 75–76.

18. Citing Bolsec, Schaff notes that Servetus' 'arrogance made him so unpopular that he had to leave Charlieu' (*History of the Christian Church*, 8:725).

Relationship to Calvin

Concerning Servetus' relationship with Calvin, they were both students at the University of Paris in the early 1530s, but there is no evidence to suggest that the two became acquainted. Although Calvin was forced to flee Paris in October 1534 (following the Placard Affair), Servetus initiated a correspondence with Calvin on doctrine.

A significant event occurred during this time of persecution when, upon Servetus' request, Calvin agreed to meet for a theological discussion in Paris. The seriousness of this cannot be overstated—Protestants were being burned alive, which was the impetus for Calvin to write his *Institutes of the Christian Religion*. At the risk of his own life, Calvin exposed himself to meet Servetus at Rue St. Antoine, but Servetus did not keep the appointment.[19]

Although Servetus offended Calvin by not meeting him in Paris, Calvin agreed to correspond with him from 1546–1548.[20] In letters that contained the early manuscripts of Servetus' final work, *The Restoration of Christianity* (1553),[21] which would prove to be primary evidence in the future trial of Servetus, he wrote to Calvin on the nature of Christ, the presence of the kingdom, and baptism.

Exhibiting behavior similar to that which he showed in Paris towards his professors, Servetus' letters contained vitriol

---

19. *CO*, 8:826. Calvin was open to dialogue with men struggling with such theological issues. One may see the same congenial spirit in Calvin's correspondences with Lelio Socin ('CCLXXXIX–To Lelio Socin,' 1551, in *John Calvin: Tracts and Letters*, vol. 1–7, edited by Jules Bonnet and translated by David Constable [Carlisle, PA: The Banner of Truth Trust, 2009], 5:330–31).

20. Calvin describes his efforts with Servetus in his 'Last Admonition to Joachim Westphal', in *John Calvin: Tracts and Letters*, edited and translated by Henry Beveridge, 2:358.

21. These letters may be found in *CO*, 8:645–714.

and condescension towards Calvin. Servetus wrote things such as: 'Very horribly you do tear God apart, blot out the true son, and fashion new gods';[22] 'the invisible gods of the Trinitarians are false, as false as the gods of the Babylonians';[23] 'I have often warned you not to admit the existence of the great and quite impossible monstrosity of the three entities in God which has no proof in any scripture properly understood …. [your] arguments are too weak for positing such a great monstrosity in God';[24] 'focus your mind briefly and I shall lead you by the hand';[25] 'wherefrom do you have dreams about so great a barbarity of a separate son in the divine generative act?';[26] 'I am plainly amazed that a man with a well-ordered mind, as you claim to be, you are cast into so deep a sea by so tiny a gust and that you would insist on clinging to so many crags and beasts';[27] 'Your illusion under the Antichrist's reign is indebted to the mesmerized Sophists who are inexperienced in the sacred tongue';[28] 'what demon has taught you … ?';[29] 'you have wholly deluded yourself';[30] 'you have not yet been born from heaven …. you … are shameless and blasphemous';[31] 'your sort of

---

22. Michael Servetus, *Thirty Letters to Calvin, Preacher to the Genevans & Sixty Signs of the Kingdom of the Antichrist and His Revelation Which Is Now at Hand*, translated by Christopher Hoffman and Marian Hillar (Lewiston, NY: Edwin Mellen Press, 2010), 1–2.
23. Ibid., 8–9.
24. Ibid., 9.
25. Ibid., 16.
26. Ibid., 27.
27. Ibid., 32.
28. Ibid., 43.
29. Ibid., 46.
30. Ibid., 49.
31. Ibid., 55.

justification is satanic';[32] 'abandon your magical delusions';[33] 'your understanding is shown to be ridiculous, nay, a magical delusion';[34] 'you are a thief and a brigand';[35] 'you wickedly confuse the times of the law and the gospel';[36] 'your ignorance is great, such that you cannot understand';[37] 'You are the most wretched of all mortals, if this demon [belief] always disturbs your own mind';[38] and 'you subvert everything and confuse heaven and earth.'[39]

Eventually, not wishing to spend time on that for which he had already written, Calvin simply sent his *Institutes* to Servetus.[40] *Quid pro quo*, Servetus returned Calvin's *Institutes* with his personal criticisms noted in the margins, along with a biting letter.[41] Characteristic of his abusive language that affected his medical career in Paris, Servetus wrote to Calvin, 'I have often told you that triad of impossible monstrosities that you admit in God is not proved by any Scriptures properly understood.'[42] He continued: 'This shows that your knowledge is ridiculous, nay, a magical enchantment and a lying justification.'[43]

Calvin was so incensed at Servetus that he wrote to William Farel (1489–1565), 'Servetus lately wrote to me, and coupled with his letter a long volume of his delirious fancies, with

---

32. Ibid., 59.
33. Ibid., 60.
34. Ibid., 62.
35. Ibid., 69.
36. Ibid., 125–26.
37. Ibid., 127–28.
38. Ibid., 135.
39. Ibid., 158.
40. *CO*, 8:487–95.
41. Ibid., 8:482–500 and 649–720.
42. Ibid., 8:653.
43. Ibid., 8:674.

the Thrasonic boast, that I should see something astonishing and unheard of. He takes it upon him to come hither, if it be agreeable to me. But I am unwilling to pledge my word for his safety, for if he shall come, I shall never permit him to depart alive, provided my authority be of any avail.[44]

While critics of Calvin cite this letter as proof of Calvin's bloodlust for Servetus, it is helpful to consider the context of Calvin's limitations in Geneva. Yale historian Bruce Gordon responds to Calvin's statement on not allowing Servetus to leave Geneva alive: 'that remark needs to be taken with a pinch of salt. Calvin could be cruel to opponents, and he did not hesitate to persecute them, but there is nothing to suggest that he actively sought to kill them.'[45] In support of Gordon's claim, it should be noted that Calvin knew of Servetus' identity and could have reported him to the Catholic authorities, but refrained. Additionally, he could have promised Servetus safe conduct to Geneva in order to trap him, but did not.

It is also helpful to review a letter of Calvin about Servetus, which was written on the same day as his letter to Farel. In this letter, Calvin expresses hope of Servetus' repentance:

> I am very ready to gratify your wishes, although I have little hope of availing anything with a man of such a disposition as he seems to possess; but yet I will try whether there is any means of bringing him to reason, which may be accomplished if God shall work an entire change in him. Since he wrote me in so haughty a tone I have wished to humble his pride, by speaking to him with a little more severity than is my custom; I could not do otherwise, for I assure you, that no lesson is

---

44. 'CLIV–To Farel,' 13 February 1546, in *John Calvin: Tracts and Letters*, 5:33. For similar sentiments concerning an anonymous heretic, see Calvin's letter, 'CCXCII–To Madame de Cany,' January 1552, in *John Calvin: Tracts and Letters*, 5:338–41.

45. Gordon, 217.

more necessary for him to learn than that of humility, which will come to him only through the influence of the Spirit of God. But still we must use our exertions for it. If God shall be so gracious to him and to us as to make this reply profitable to him, I shall have occasion for joy.[46]

Consequently, it is likely that Calvin's comments to Farel were born in anger and, while not representing a pursuit to have Servetus executed, give insight into Calvin's future support of Servetus' execution. As will be shown below, the pastors of Geneva had no such power. This authority resided only with the secular state.

As a result of Servetus' persistent 'incorrigible obstinacy' towards orthodox doctrine, Calvin refused to continue writing in order to 'comply with what Paul mentions' (possibly a reference to Titus 3:10).[47] Servetus continued to write Calvin some thirty times, but with no reply.[48] Not satisfied with Calvin's silence, Servetus turned his wrath on Calvin's fellow minister in Geneva, Abel Poupin. In his characteristic style, Servetus wrote:

Your gospel is without God, without true faith, without good works. Instead of a God you have a three-headed Cerberus. For faith you have a deterministic dream, and good works you say

---

46. 'CLIII–To John Frellon,' 13 February 1546, in *John Calvin: Tracts and Letters*, 5:30–31. In this letter, Calvin wrote under the pseudonym, 'Charles d'Espeville.' Calvin wrote of this hope: 'For God, whenever it pleases him, changes the worst men into the best, engrafts the alien, and adopts the stranger into the church' (*Institutes of the Christian Religion*, 2 volumes, edited by John T. McNeill and translated by Ford Lewis Battles [Louisville, KY: Westminster John Knox Press, 1960], 2:1237).

47. 'VI–To Viret,' 1 September 1548, in *John Calvin: Tracts and Letters*, 7:409.

48. Servetus' continued correspondences may be found in *CO*, 8:645–714.

are inane pictures. With you the faith of Christ is mere deceit effecting nothing. Man is with you an inert trunk, and God is a chimera of the enslaved will …. You close the Kingdom of Heaven before men … Woe! Woe! Woe! This is the third letter that I have written to warn you that you may know better. I will not warn you again. Perhaps it will offend you that I meddle in this fight of Michael [the Archangel against Satan] and wish to involve you. Study that passage carefully and you will see that they are men who will fight there, giving their souls to death in blood and for a testimony to Jesus Christ …. I know that I shall certainly die on this account, but I do not falter that I may be a disciple like the Master.[49]

As a foreshadowing of things to come, Servetus would die for his doctrine.

---

49. *CO*, 8:750-1, quoted in Bainton, *Hunted Heretic*, 99.

2

SERVETUS' ARREST AND ESCAPE FROM VIENNE

Servetus' Arrest in Vienne

Servetus published *The Restoration of Christianity* in January 1553, which sharply criticized the Trinity, orthodox Christology, original sin, and infant baptism.[1] Servetus believed he was revealing that which was long hidden about God when he

---

1. The full title is, *The Restoration of Christianity. A calling of the whole apostolic church to make a fresh start, restored completely in the knowledge of God, the faith of Christ, our justification, regeneration, baptism, and the Lord's Supper. Our restoration finally in the kingdom of heaven, with the loosing of the captivity of ungodly Babylon and Antichrist and his own destroyed.* The Latin title of this work (*Christianismi Restitutio*) resembled that of Calvin's *Institutes of the Christian Religion* (*Institutio Christianae Religionis*) and was perceived to be a mockery of Calvin's work. One could also interpret the title as an appeal to Humanist and Anabaptist communities, who would have been drawn to the idea of restitution to a more pure form of ancient Christianity.

wrote, 'We shall now see God, unseen before …. It is high time to open this door and this way of the light, without which no one can read the sacred Scriptures, or know God, or become a Christian.'[2] When the work reached Geneva, Calvin and his associates immediately recognized the content as originating from the pen of Servetus.

A turning point occurred early in 1553 when Guillaume de Trie, a merchant from Lyon and friend of Calvin, wrote Antoine Arneys, his Catholic cousin living in Lyon.[3] De Trie had suffered ridicule from his family for converting to Protestantism, so he was eager to boastfully write to his cousin concerning the doctrinal purity of the Protestant cause in comparison to that of the Catholics. He decried that Catholics were tolerating a heretic who was under the employment of the Archbishop himself. In a letter dated 26 February 1553, de Trie identified Servetus as Villenueva, identified his publisher (Balthazar Arnoullet), and sent the first four leaves of *The Restoration* as proof.[4]

De Trie's cousin passed on the information to the Catholic authorities who then conducted an investigation under the inquisitor of Vienne, Matthieu Ory (1492–1557). Servetus was summoned to court on 16 March, but no evidence could be found at Servetus' home or at the printing press of Arnoullet.

Schaff writes concerning Servetus' heresies in this book: 'To his contemporaries the *Restitutio* appeared to be a confused compound of Sabellian, Samosatenic, Arian, Apollianarian, and Pelagian heresies, mixed with Anabaptist errors and Neo-platonic, pantheistic speculations. The best judges—Calvin, Saisset, Trechsel, Baur, Dorner, Harnack—find the root of his system in pantheism.' In Schaff's assessment, 'Servetus was a mystic theosophist and Christopantheist' (*History of the Christian Church*, 8:736–37).

2. Ibid., 8:734.

3. He would write three letters, which are found in *CO*, 8:835–38, 840–44.

4. *CO*, 8:835–8. Here Calvin explicitly denies taking part in the writing of Guillaume de Trie's letters.

Ory then requested Calvin's correspondences from de Trie, which prompted Servetus' arrest on 4 April 1553.

In a letter that gives insight into Calvin's motives, de Trie described the difficulty of procuring the incriminating letters from Calvin:

> I can tell you I had no little trouble to get from Calvin what I am sending. Not that he does not wish to repress such execrable blasphemies, but he thinks his duty is rather to convince heretics with doctrine than with other means, because he does not exercise the sword of justice.[5] But I pressured him, remonstrating and pointing out the embarrassing position in which I should be placed if he did not help me, so that in the end he gave me what you see.[6]

This evidence further supports the claim that Calvin was not intent on pursuing and executing Servetus, but converting him to the truth.[7]

Servetus was interrogated three times in two days, and under oath falsified his true identity. While Servetus was in

---

5. Calvin writes in his *Institutes*, 'this is the aim of ecclesiastical jurisdiction: that offenses be resisted, and any scandal that has arisen be wiped out. In its use two things ought to be taken into account: that this spiritual power be completely separated from the right of the sword; secondly, that it be administered not by the decision of one man but by a lawful assembly .... For the severest punishment of the church, the final thunderbolt, so to speak, is excommunication, which is used only in necessity' (2:1217). Also, 'Paul's course of action for excommunicating a man is the lawful one, provided the elders do not do it by themselves alone, but with the knowledge and approval of the church; in this way the multitude of the people does not decide the action but observes as witness and guardian so that nothing may be done according to the whim of a few' (Ibid., 2:1235).

6. *CO*, 8:842.

7. Calvin writes, 'For, in excommunication the intent is to lead the sinner to repentance and to remove bad examples from the midst, lest either Christ's name be maligned or others be provoked to imitate them' (*Institutes*, 2:1236).

custody during his trial, he took advantage of the freedoms he was given (as a result of his status in society as a physician) and escaped on 7 April 1553. Regardless, the court of Vienne passed its sentence on 17 June 1553 and ruled that Servetus was to be burned alive with a slow fire, until his body be reduced to ashes. He was hung and burned in effigy with five bales of paper which represented his books.[8] The entirety of the sentence from the Vienne court was later delivered to Geneva as proof of Servetus' conviction, and as evidence that he should be delivered back to Vienne to carry out the sentence of execution by fire.

The Context of Execution in Sixteenth Century Europe

The history of execution by fire extends back to antiquity. Proponents of execution by burning the condemned note that it was practiced prior to the giving of the Decalogue (Gen. 38:24), was made official in the Law of Moses (Lev. 20:14; 21:9), and was (and will be) practiced by God Himself as a form of execution in the Old Testament and New Testament (Lev. 10:2; Num. 16:35; and Rev. 20:9). This form of punishment has been practiced by many cultures, and continued through Roman times under the birth of Christianity.

Notable figures such as Theodosius the Great (347–395), Jerome (347–420), Augustine (354–430), Leo I (400–461), Aquinas (1225–1274), and Erasmus of Rotterdam (1466–1536) promoted execution for heresy. Following Augustine, the Codex of Justinian and Carolingian Law made execution legal in cases of Trinitarian heresy and also commended death by fire for religious violations.[9] While there were periodic objections

---

8.   *CO*, 8:784–87.

9.   *The Codex of Justinian* 1.9.3, 1.5.8.11, and 1.6.2. http://uwdigital.uwyo. edu/islandora/object/wyu:12399. Accessed 25 October 2016. Roland

to execution in general, and burning in particular, these laws became standard and were accepted in Christendom.[10]

Theodosius the Great, the enforcer of Nicene orthodoxy in the Empire, was the first to practice capital punishment for certain types of Christian heresy. Emperor Maximus (335–388) applied these principles to Priscillian (Manichaean) and ordered six followers to be tortured and beheaded (386).

Augustine is arguably the most influential early theologian in Church history and had a monumental impact upon Calvin. The 1559 edition of Calvin's *Institutes* contains over two hundred citations from Augustine. While believing that those who persecute the Church by martyring the faithful should not be put to death, Augustine argued for the use of force against heresy. He did this based upon New and Old Testament evidence (Gal. 4:22–31 [Sarah was a type of the Church and she cruelly treated her handmaid]; Ps. 18:37), as well as personal testimony to the effectiveness of such means, if done in love. He wrote: 'there is a righteous persecution, which the Church of Christ inflicts upon the impious,' but in contrast to pagans who persecute out of hatred, the Church 'persecutes in the spirit of love' in order to correct and recall from error, with the goal of leading the one in error to eternal salvation.[11]

Bainton writes concerning these two charges: 'Both these offenses were punishable by death in the Roman law, the great code of Justinian which was then enjoying a revival in western Europe' ('Burned Heretic: Michael Servetus' in *The Christian Century* [28 October 1953; 1230–1231], 1230). Although the law was not strictly followed in Geneva, it was consulted in matters concerning the Consistory. For example, see *Registers of the Consistory of Geneva in the Time of Calvin*. Volume 1:1542–44 (Grand Rapids: Eerdmans, 2000), 326.

10. See Brad S. Gregory, *Salvation at Stake: Christian Martyrdom in Early Modern Europe* (Cambridge, MA: Harvard University Press, 1999), 75–96.

11. 'A Treatise Concerning the Correction of the Donatists; or Epistle CLXXXV' in *Nicene and Post-Nicene Fathers*, edited by Philip Schaff, first series (Peabody, MA: Hendrickson, 1999), 4:637.

According to Augustine, 'chastising with religious severity' is to be directed by kings (exemplified by Hezekiah, Josiah, Darius, and Nebuchadnezzar), out of fear of the Lord (Ps. 2:1–2, 10–11).[12]

Augustine recognizes the tension between compulsion by fear on the one hand and persuasion by words on the other, but concludes that more are corrected by fear than love. His primary evidence was the Apostle Paul who was first dashed to the earth and struck with blindness before the Lord saved him. Augustine wrote, 'For it is wonderful how he who entered the service of the gospel in the first instance under the compulsion of bodily punishment, afterwards labored more in the gospel than all they who were called by word only; and he who was compelled by the greater influence of fear to love, displayed that perfect love which casts out fear.'[13]

Jerome agreed with his contemporary Augustine by appealing to Deuteronomy 13:6–10, the javelin of Phinehas (Num. 25:7–8), 'Peter in putting to death Ananias and Sapphira' (see Acts 5:1–10), and Paul in dooming Elymas to a time of blindness (Acts 13:8–11). He explained what should be done to one who does not believe in the veneration of martyrs' relics: 'The wretch's tongue should be cut out,' and 'There is no cruelty in regard for God's honour.'[14]

Leo I, one of the most powerful early popes, said by Calvin to be 'the last bishop of Rome,'[15] agreed to the execution of the

---

12. Ibid., 640.

13. Ibid., 641–2. Augustine also appeals to Paul's words: 'Having in a readiness to revenge all disobedience, when your obedience is fulfilled' (see 2 Cor. 10:6) and Jesus who said, 'compel them to come in' (Luke 14:23).

14. 'Letter CIX: To Riparius' in *Nicene and Post-Nicene Fathers*, edited by Philip Schaff and Henry Wace, second series (Peabody, MA: Hendrickson, 1999), 6:212–14.

15. *Institutes*, 2:1427.

Priscillians and promoted execution for heresy. Following Leo I, the Codex of Justinian (*Corpus Juris Civilis*) made execution legal in cases of Trinitarian heresy and also commended death by fire for religious violations (mid-sixth century).[16]

These laws became standard and accepted in Christendom. In the Medieval Period burnings were rare, but seen in cases such as Orléans in 1022 and affirmed in 1148 by the Council of Rheims. The Eastern Church also practiced executions, even burning at the stake. A notable example is that of Avvakum Petrov (1620–82) who was burned alive for opposing reforms in the Russian Orthodox Church.

These policies were supported by the leading theologian of the Medieval Period, Thomas Aquinas. He wrote,

> *I answer that,* With regard to heretics two points must be observed: one, on their own side; the other, on the side of the Church. On their own side there is the sin, whereby they deserve not only to be separated from the Church by excommunication, but also to be severed from the world by death. For it is a much graver matter to corrupt the faith which quickens the soul, than to forge money, which supports temporal life. Wherefore if forgers of money and other evil-doers are forthwith condemned to death by the secular authority, much more reason is there for heretics, as soon as they are convicted of heresy, to be not only excommunicated but even put to death.[17]

---

16. Codex of Justinian I.V.8.11, I.VI.2 and I.IX.3. Justinian I (483–565) was Byzantine Emperor from 527–65. The Codex of Justinian (527–34) condemned heretics for denial of the Trinity and repetition of baptism (Anabaptism), which was what Servetus was executed for (*CO*, 8:827–29).

17. *Summa Theologica,* Benziger Bros./Accordance electronic ed. 3 vols. (Altamonte Springs: OakTree Software, 2004), paragraph 15237. II–II.11.3.

Perhaps the most famous burning leading up to the Reformation was of John Hus (1369–1415). Promised safe conduct by Sigismund of Hungary (1368–1437), Hus was condemned as a heretic at the Council of Constance (1414–1418) and was burned in light of the Council's decision that promise of safe conduct should not apply to heretics. This also resulted in the exhumation, grinding, and burning of the bones of Hus' theological mentor, John Wycliffe (c. 1328–1384).

Moving into the time of the Reformation, Erasmus of Rotterdam, known for his irenic spirit, concurred with his predecessors to the point of burning the condemned: 'I would agree that an extremely contumacious heretic might be burned.'[18] One of Martin Luther's (1483–1546) debate partners, Johann Eck (1486–1543), with whom he famously debated in Heidelberg (1519), gives evidence to the true danger in which Luther found himself at a time when he was officially excommunicated from the Catholic Church. Eck confirms this practice in his chapter, 'Concerning the Burning of Heretics' in his book, *Enchiridion of Commonplaces: Against Luther and Other Enemies of the Church* (1525).[19]

Unable at that time to distinguish between utopian, anti-Trinitarian (rational), and moderate forms of Anabaptism, councils like the Diet of Speyer (1529) interpreted all Anabaptists to be of the radical utopian strain, and imposed the death penalty for all Anabaptists based upon Justinian law. This Diet gained the approval of Emperor Charles V (1500–1558) and was sanctioned as the Carolingian Law (*Constitutio Criminalis Carolina*), which was later agreed upon in 1530 at

---

18. Quoted in Roland H. Bainton, *Erasmus of Christendom* (New York: Charles Scribner's Sons, 1969), 203.

19. Translated by Ford Lewis Battles (Grand Rapids: Baker Book House, 1979), 178–85.

the Diet of Augsburg. It was then ratified in 1532 at the Diet of Regensburg when it became official law.

While many more examples could be given, during the reign of Mary I of England (1516–1558), famously known as 'Bloody Mary,' nearly 300 Protestants were burned for their faith.[20] Of importance in the trial of Servetus, the French inquisitor, Matthieu Ory, who arrested Servetus justified these acts when he wrote,

> If then, dead books may be committed to the flames [Acts 19:19], how much more live books, that is to say, men? Scripture says that a witch should not be allowed to live and heretics are spiritual witches. The law of nature enjoins that a corrupted member be amputated. The tares, of course, were not to be rooted out in Christ's day when the rulers were not yet Christian. The case is altered now.[21]

Apart from Catholic and Eastern Orthodox voices, Protestants also participated in executions, although to a much lesser extent.[22] Following Servetus' execution, the city of Bern beheaded Giovanni Valentino Gentile (1520–1566) for his anti-Trinitarian views.[23] Huldrych Zwingli (1484–1531) condoned the drowning of Anabaptists and employed torture to acquire information from prisoners. He wrote concerning the Anabaptists: 'Whoever will be baptized hereafter will be

---

20. Gregory, *Salvation at Stake*, 92.

21. Bainton, *Hunted Heretic*, 52.

22. As an example of the difference between Catholic and Protestant persecution, no Protestant can come close to the statistics of the Spanish inquisitor, Tomás de Torquemada (1420–1498), who is purported to have burned approximately 8,800 people for various crimes and tortured 90,000 in sundry ways (Schaff, *History of the Christian Church*, 8:689).

23. E. William Monter, *Calvin's Geneva* (Eugene, OR: Wipf & Stock, 1967), 83–84.

submerged permanently …. I was once deeply grieved by the incorrigible audacity of these people. Now I am greatly irked by it.'[24]

Thomas Cranmer (1489–1556) encouraged young Edward VI (1537–1553) to sign the death warrants of Joan Bocher of Kent and George Van Pare, who were both burned on 2 May 1550. Queen Elizabeth I (1533–1603) of England employed one of the most brutal execution devices of all time: being drawn, hung and quartered.[25] Even in Œcolampadius' Basel, where Servetus was tolerated for a time and expelled, Konrad in der Gassen was executed for heresy in 1530 (the same year Servetus resided in Basel).

When the utopian strain of Anabaptism was causing chaos under the spiritual leadership of Thomas Müntzer (1489–1525), the Protestant Philip of Hesse (1504–1567) led the charge which left over six thousand dead at the Battle of Frankenhausen (May 1525).[26] In April 1525, just prior to the massacre, Luther agreed to the right of the state to administer justice in his, *Against the Murderous, Thieving Hordes of Peasants*. In this work, Luther admonishes the authorities: 'Stab, smite, slay, whoever can. If you die in doing it, well for you! A more blessed death can never be yours, for you die obeying the divine Word and

---

24. Zwingli to Vadian, 7 March 1526, *Huldreich Zwinglis sämtliche Werke*, edited by Fritz Blanke (Zürich: Verlag Berichthaus, 1968), VIII.542. Quoted in Leland Harder, 'Zwingli's Reaction to the Schleitheim Confession of Faith of the Anabaptists' in *Sixteenth Century Journal* XI:4 (1980), 52.

25. This entailed being dragged behind a horse to the place of execution. Once there, the victim is repeatedly hung so as to torture, but not to kill. The victim is then placed on a slab where he is castrated and has his entrails cut out. His body parts are then burned before his eyes while he is still alive. Finally, the victim is quartered and beheaded. These types of executions were used by Protestants in England from 1585 until 1681.

26. Lyndal Roper, *Martin Luther: Renegade and Prophet* (New York: Random House, 2017), 254.

commandment in Romans XIII, and in loving service of your neighbor, whom you are rescuing from the bonds of hell and of the devil.'[27]

Luther would be even more explicit concerning God's involvement in these matters: 'It is not man, but God who hangs, tortures, beheads, kills and fights. All these are God's works and judgments.'[28] Luther also implicitly gave his approval to the execution of Anabaptists according to the judgment of the Diet of Speyer in 1529.[29] The last execution by burning in

---

27. *Luther's Works* [LW], 55 volumes. Edited and translated by Theodore G. Tappert, general editors Helmut T. Lehmann and Jaroslav Pelikan (Philadelphia: Fortress Press and Concordia, 1900–1986), 46:54–55.

28. 'Whether Soldiers, Too, May Be Saved' (1526) in *LW*, 46:96.

29. There was an official protest against the Diet of Speyer, also in 1529, and despite the fact that the Protestants argued against several points, they were clear that they did not oppose the condemnation of Anabaptists to execution. The protestors said that the Diet's ruling on the Anabaptists was in every respect proper. The following significant figures of the Reformation, being close confidants of Luther, were signatories to this ruling: Elector John of Saxony, Margrave George of Brandenburg, the dukes Ernst and Franz of Braunschweig-Lüneburg, Landgrave Philipp of Hesse, Prince Wolfgang of Anhalt; and the imperial cities of Strasbourg, Nuremberg, Ulm, Constance, Lindau, Memmingen, Kempten, Nördlingen, Heilbronn, Reutlingen, Isny, St. Gall, Weissenburg, and Windsheim.

Evaluating Luther, although he approved of executing heretics, he did distinguish between heretics that were radical and revolutionary (utopian Anabaptists) and those who simply held theological heresy. It must also be noted that Luther said, 'To burn heretics is contrary to the will of the Holy Spirit,' and 'False teachers should not be put to death; it is enough to banish them' (conclusion LXXX in 'Resolution on Indulgences' [1518] and 'Letter to Link' [1528]). It is a matter of conjecture concerning how Luther would rule on someone like Servetus, but there is good evidence that he would have supported execution for obstinate or seditious heretics (see Roland Bainton, *Here I Stand: A Life of Martin Luther* [New York: Penguin Books, 1995], 295–56). Luther mentions Servetus once in his Table Talk, referring to Servetus' *De Trinitatis Errobibus* as 'an exceedingly virulent book,' but without further judgment. *LW* 54:32. See also, Eike Wolgast, 'Speyer, Protestation of' in *The Oxford Encyclopedia of the Reformation*,

England took place at the command of King James I (1566–1625), who had executed Edward Wightman in 1612.

Protestant confessions also testify to this nearly universal opinion concerning heresy. Following the Belgic Confession (1561), which stated that the magistrates 'may remove and prevent all idolatry and false worship, that the kingdom of antichrist may be thus destroyed and the kingdom of Christ promoted,'[30] the Second Helvetic Confession (1566) admonishes the Magistracy, 'let him draw forth this sword of God [Rom. 13:4] against all malefactors, seditious persons, thieves or murderers, oppressors, blasphemers, perjured persons, and all those whom God has commanded him to punish or even to execute. Let him suppress stubborn heretics (which are heretics indeed), who cease not to blaspheme the majesty of God, and to trouble the Church, yes, and finally to destroy it.'[31] This became the basis for the Hungarian Reformed communion in their 'Documents of the Debrecen Synod' (1567), which, after citing with approval the executions of Servetus and Gentile, state that the Magistracy 'may be able to remove heretics and their insufferable wickedness from the city of God.'[32] Furthermore, 'We teach, in accordance with the Word of God, that blasphemers and heretics that have been lawfully refuted and condemned by true doctrine are mortal sinners who must be ejected from the church and put to death by the law of the

---

4 volumes, edited by Hans. J. Hillerbrand (New York: Oxford University Press, 1996), 4:103–05.

30. *Reformed Confessions of the 16th and 17th Centuries in English Translation*, 4 volumes, compiled with introductions by James T. Dennison, Jr. (Grand Rapids: Reformation Heritage Books, 2010), 2:447–8. As it relates to the Calvinist/Arminian controversy, this is the Confession that Jacob Arminius (1560–1609) would have subscribed to as an employee of the state (pastor).

31. Ibid., 2:880.

32. Ibid., 3:11 (cf. 3:62). See also this document's, 'A Response to the Arguments of the Followers of Servetus,' 3:27–41.

sword by the magistrates. Such are the followers of Sabellius, Servetus, Arius, and Photinus, who deny the true Trinity ....'[33]

The Westminster Confession of Faith (1646) touches on this subject as well, stating:

> The civil magistrate ... hath authority, and it is his duty, to take order that unity and peace be preserved in the Church, that the truth of God be kept pure and entire, that all blasphemies and heresies be suppressed all corruptions and abuses in worship and discipline prevented or reformed, and all the ordinances of God duly settled, administered, and observed.[34]

Forms of punishment, torture and execution are uncomfortable topics for the modern reader, and often result in anachronistic judgments by the best of historians. However, the distaste for and elimination of the death penalty would have been quite foreign to those living in the sixteenth century. In their time, it was a legitimate, lawful way to punish heretics to prevent them from spreading heresy, and to discourage others from imitating their doctrine. Bainton describes the understanding of French parliament against heresy:

> Heresy is the supreme crime because it is lèse majesté against the divine sovereign, because it destroys souls for eternity rather than merely shortening life in the body. It is worse than matricide because it rends the Holy Mother Church, the Immaculate Bride of Christ. It is worse than treason because it breaks the bond of civil society and disintegrates Christendom; it is worse than counterfeiting because it devaluates the

---

33. Ibid., 3:133 (the death penalty is justified from Scripture as well: 3:134–35). See also 'The Confession of La Rochelle' (1571) that admonishes the magistrates 'to suppress the sins committed not only against the second table of the commandments of God, but also against the first' (3:322), and 'The Hungarian *Confessio Catholica*' (1562), 2:544.

34. Ibid., 4:114.

truth of God. If thieves be impaled, homicides beheaded, counterfeiters burned in oil, and parricides consumed in acid, shall we then spare these pseudo-Evangelical Lutherans whose crime exceeds parricide? …. Severity is an ultimate kindness; just as the amputation of a putrid member may save a body, so the stake may turn tares into wheat or may protect the wheat from the insidious scab. Have not the great Christian emperors, Theodosius, Justinian, and Charlemagne, placed their swords at the service of the Church?[35]

Additionally, those who began to oppose execution—the Anabaptists—were considered dangerous and revolutionary, which would make their views on execution suspect as an attempt to spread their views.[36]

While statistics are being refined, it has been estimated that 3,000 people were executed in Europe for heresy during the time of the Reformation (two-thirds were Anabaptists) and over 30,000 were executed for witchcraft.[37] It should be noted that a vast majority of these were committed by the Catholic Church through her various inquisitions.

Regardless, the evidence clearly shows that Catholics, Orthodox, and Protestants all participated in heresy executions and justified it by appealing to Scripture. As Richard Gamble

---

35. Quoted in Bainton, *Hunted Heretic*, 50–51.

36. Balthasar Hubmaier, 'On Heretics and Those Who Burn Them', in *Balthasar Hubmaier: Theologian of Anabaptism*, translated and edited by H. Wayne Pipkin and John H. Yoder, 58–66. Classics of the Radical Reformation, vol. 5 (Scottdale, PA: Herald, 1989). Concerning those who opposed the death penalty at the time, Schaff writes, 'The only advocates of toleration in the sixteenth century were Anabaptists and Antitrinitarians, who were themselves sufferers from persecution' (*History of the Christian Church*, 8:711). While this is not entirely accurate, critics were in the severe minority.

37. William Monter, 'Heresy Executions in Reformation Europe, 1520–1565', in *Tolerance and Intolerance in the European Reformation*, edited by Ole Peter Greek and Bob Scribner (New York: Cambridge University Press, 1996), 49, 63.

writes, 'In the sixteenth century, no enlightened civil leader believed that the government did not have the right to execute blasphemers and heretics ....'[38] In short, 'Tolerance ... did not exist in the sixteenth century. In fact, it appeared impious.'[39]

The Context of Execution in Sixteenth Century Geneva

While the previously mentioned law codes governed the Holy Roman Empire, one must question whether or not Catholics and Protestants prosecuted crime in the same manner. As mentioned above, there is a significant discrepancy in numbers of those who suffered execution by Catholics and Protestants. There is no doubt that both groups upheld execution for heresy, but was there consistency in the application of the law? Were there cases of grace and leniency, or were all heretics immediately executed as a threat to Christian unity?

There were cases of abuse, but in general, the one accused of heresy in Protestantism and Catholicism was given ample time for contemplation, prayer, counsel, and repentance. The goal was restoration, not death. In fact, the execution of a heretic was largely thought to be a failure on the part of the religious majority to persuade the person to recant. Also, in numerous cases the Imperial law was not followed. Sentences of crimes that were punishable by death according to the law were often lessened to physical punishment, expulsion from the city of residence, or monetary fines.

---

38. 'Calvin's Controversies,' *The Cambridge Companion to John Calvin* (ed. Donald K. McKim; Cambridge: Cambridge University Press, 2004), 198.

39. Bernard Cottrett, *Calvin: A Biography*, translated by M. Wallace McDonald (Grand Rapids: Eerdmans, 1995), 207.

While those sympathetic to Geneva's actions against Servetus have appealed to these laws as a necessity for the death sentence, it must also be recognized that there is some degree of uncertainty on whether or not these laws were the sole foundation of justice in Geneva.[40]

While the previously mentioned law codes governed the Holy Roman Empire, it must be recognized that the law was not consistently practiced in most cities of the time, including Geneva.[41] Specifically, anti-Trinitarianism and Anabaptism, both crimes of which Servetus was guilty, and both of which were punishable by death under Imperial law, were not universally punished by execution in Geneva before or after Servetus' execution.

As a window into the use of Imperial law in Geneva, Calvin described the errors of Giovanni Valentino Gentile (1520–1566) as scarcely different than Servetus, that he covered Calvin with 'many scurrilous outrages,' and that he displayed

---

40. William Monter writes, 'we know a good deal about the history of legislation, but next to nothing about how this legislation was really enforced during the age of the Reformation. This generalization applies with full force to the history of Calvin's Geneva, where discussions of judicial practice have not yet risen above the level of polemic' ('Crime and Punishment in Calvin's Geneva, 1562' in *Archiv für Reformationsgeschichte* 64 [1973]), 281. While more light has been shed on this issue since Monter wrote, this issue continues to be a question regarding Servetus.

41. Monter writes, 'Many accounts of Calvin's Geneva, wishing to illustrate the unbelievable severity of her justice, point to a five-year span in which 58 people were executed and 76 banished. Yet all the crimes for which capital sentence was pronounced were also punishable by death in the famous *Constitutio Criminalis Carolina* promulgated earlier in the reign of Charles V by the Diet of Regensburg in 1532. Thirty-eight of Geneva's executions were for witchcraft or for spreading the plague, which the *Carolina* punished with hideous tortures and executions' (*Calvin's Geneva*, 152–3). See especially sections 105–6 in the *Constitutio Criminalis Carolina*. See also Scott M. Manetsch, *Calvin's Company of Pastors: Pastoral Care and the Emerging Reformed Church, 1536–1609* (New York: Oxford University Press, 2013).

'pride, malice, hypocrisy, and obstinate impudence.'[42] Schaff writes the following concerning this Genevan heresy trial in 1557: 'The Council asked the judgment of five lawyers, who decided that, according to the Imperial laws (*De summa Trinitate et fide catholica et de hereticis*) Gentile deserved death by fire. The Council, instead, pronounced the milder sentence of death by the sword.'[43] Gentile's sentence was commuted, however, following his recantation and agreement to the 'Confession of Faith Set Forth in the Italian Church of Geneva (18 May 1558).[44] Following a humiliating period of penance, he left Geneva only to recant of his recantation, and later was beheaded in Bern (10 September 1566).

Matteo Gribaldi (1505–1564), also an anti-Trinitarian, was a frequent visitor to Geneva. Gribaldi was present at the initial stages of Servetus' trial, but took leave to Basel before its conclusion.[45] Gribaldi would return to Geneva, which resulted in his arrest for heretical opinions. Yet, despite Gribaldi's refusal to repent of his doctrine, and confessing his alliance with Servetus, he was not burned in Geneva but was expelled from the city in 1558 following a recantation.[46]

---

42. 'DIV–To the Marquis de Vico,' 19 July 1558, in *John Calvin: Tracts and Letters*, 6:443.

43. Schaff, *History of the Christian Church*, 8:656.

44. In *Reformed Confessions of the 16th and 17th Centuries*, 3:114–16; cf. *CO*, 9:385–8. Calvin wrote the following work against him: *An Exposition of the Impiety of Valentino Gentilis* (*Expositio impietatis Valentini Gentilis*). See *CO*, 9:368–70 and Robert Letham's translation in *The Holy Trinity: In Scripture, History, Theology, and Worship* (Phillipsburg, NJ: P&R, 2004), 262. Cf. Beza, 'The Life of John Calvin,' 1:lxxix.

45. Gordon, 225; Schaff, *History of the Christian Church*, 8:653.

46. Ronald Wallace, *Calvin, Geneva and the Reformation* (Eugene, OR: Wipf & Stock, 1998), 296; 'DI–To Nicholas Zerkinden,' 4 July 1558, in *John Calvin: Tracts and Letters*, 6:431.

An additional anti-Trinitarian in Geneva was Italian physician, Giorgio Biandrata (1515–1588).[47] Calvin met with him, wrote to him extensively and even gave him a promise of safe conduct in Geneva. Biandrata eventually fled the city in 1558 after living in the city for a year.[48]

Immediately prior to the arrest of Servetus (13 August), Jean Bodin/Baudin (1529/30–1596) was expelled from Geneva for his belief that Jesus was a ghost.[49]

Giovanni Alciati (1515–1573), a military officer from Milan, was a member of the Italian church in Geneva.[50] Aware of brewing anti-Trinitarianism in the Italian congregation, the pastors of Geneva held an open meeting with the Italians on 18 May 1558 where they were told they could speak freely about their opinions. Schaff records that 'Alciati went so far as to declare that the orthodox party "worshipped three devils worse than all the idols of popery."'[51] Despite such blasphemy, Alciati was not arrested, tried or executed. Time was given for them to reconsider their position, and during that interval he fled the city.[52]

---

47. Also spelled 'Biandrata.' Schaff mentions that an Italian church was started by 1542 in Geneva (*History of the Christian Church*, 8:629). Cf. Theodore Beza, 'The Life of John Calvin', in *John Calvin: Tracts and Letters*, 1:lxxix. Following this debacle, the Italian Church of Geneva published a statement of faith that was explicitly Trinitarian ('Confession of the Italian Church of Geneva' [1558]), 111–16.

48. Wallace, 296; see also the letter of Calvin: 'DIV–To the Marquis de Vico,' which includes a condemnation of Biandrata's anti-Trinitarian views (19 July 1558, in *John Calvin: Tracts and Letters*, 6:442) (see also fn. 3).

49. William G. Naphy, *Calvin and the Consolidation of the Genevan Reformation* (Louisville KY: Westminster John Knox Press, 2003), 183.

50. Ibid.

51. Schaff, *History of the Christian Church*, 8:655.

52. Selderhuis, *John Calvin: A Pilgrim's Life* (Downers Grove, IL: IVP Academic, 2009), 215; Schaff, *History of the Christian Church*, 8:655.

Italians were not the only anti-Trinitarians in Geneva. Polish by birth, anti-Trinitarian Lelio Sozzini/Socini (1525–1562) also frequently visited Geneva without being arrested, and had extensive correspondences with Calvin.[53] Finally, Antoine Pellinque also denied the Trinity in Geneva and was excommunicated on 15 February 1560.[54] These accounts are important because they follow the trial of Servetus and the publication of Calvin's *Defense of the Orthodox Faith against the Monstrous Errors of the Spaniard Michael Servetus* (1554) where Calvin defended the judgment against Servetus.[55]

As for Servetus, 'The Council had no doubt of its jurisdiction in the case; it had to respect the unanimous judgment of the Churches, the public horror of heresy and blasphemy, and the Imperial laws of Christendom, which were appealed to by the attorney-general. The decision was unanimous.'[56] Even Rilliet, who gave the official report on the trial (and was not an avid supporter of Calvin), wrote that the sentence was 'odious before our consciences, but was just according to the law.'[57]

Consequently, original documents indicate that Imperial law was respected and appealed to when needed, while the local ordinances were followed for logistics.[58] As a result of the

---

53. Selderhuis, *John Calvin: A Pilgrim's Life*, 217.

54. Manetsch, 364, fn. 63. Manetsch discovered this in the unpublished volumes of the *Registres du Consistoire*, 1551–1609 in the Archiv d'État de Genève (17 [1560], 7).

55. Known in the original as, *Defensio orthodoxae fidei, contra prodigiosos errores Michaelis Serveti Hispani*, this work has never been translated into English.

56. Schaff, *History of the Christian Church*, 8:781.

57. Ibid., 8:782.

58. These ordinances are: Ecclesiastical Ordinances (1541), Edict of the Lieutenant (1542), and the Ordinances on Offices and Officers (1543). The Edict of the Lieutenant and the Ordinances on Offices and Officers can be found in vol. 2 of *Les Sources du Droit du Canton de Genève*, 1930. A partial translation of the Ordinances on Offices

review of these cases, it is evident that anti-Trinitarians were not universally executed in Geneva.[59] Reminiscent of Augustine, Calvin wrote, '[concerning] judicial law, surely every nation is left free to make such laws as it foresees to be profitable to itself .... in conformity to that perpetual rule of love ....'[60] While Imperial law was used as a basis for the punishment of crime, each case was reviewed individually by the magistrates.

Comparing Geneva to the rest of Europe at this time, William Monter writes, 'The only certain conclusion is that Geneva executed nobody for reasons which sixteenth-century Imperial law (to which Geneva may or may not have been subject) would have considered unusual.'[61]

Does this evidence then prove that Calvin had a vendetta against Servetus because of their personal history? Is it true that Calvin overlooked other heretics, but was blinded by his hatred of Servetus to the point of murder? Although this is not an uncommon charge against Calvin, it is not supported by the evidence. In fact, the evidence will show that Servetus likely would not have been executed in Geneva if it were not for two critical factors.

---

and Officers can be found in John Witte, Jr. and Robert M. Kingdon, *Sex, Marriage, and Family Life in John Calvin's Geneva: Courtship, Engagement, and Marriage* (Grand Rapids: Eerdmans, 2005), 80–87.

59. These cases also refute the notion by popular authors such as Earle Cairns that Servetus was executed simply because he 'questioned the doctrine of the Trinity' (*Christianity Through the Centuries* [Grand Rapids: Zondervan], 311).

60. *Institutes,* 2:1503.

61. *Calvin's Geneva,* 153.

3

THE AUTHORITY OF JOHN CALVIN IN GENEVA

Calvin is popularly portrayed as the 'Pope of Geneva' who imposed himself upon all aspects of city life and government. As a result, it is important to inquire into the extent of Calvin's control during the trial of Michael Servetus.

Part of the answer involves Calvin's legal status in the city of Geneva. There were three classes of people in Geneva: (1) *Citoyens* were born in Geneva by Genevan parents; (2) *Bourgeois* were those of a privileged position, but could not serve on the all-important Small Council; and (3) *Habitants* were foreigners who were basically legal, resident aliens who did not have the right to vote, sit on a city council, or even to carry a weapon.

As a Frenchman, Calvin was a *habitant* who was essentially a missionary relegated to the lowest status in Genevan society.

He did not dominate the city, he held no public office, he was not a citizen (thus, he could not vote in elections), and he was constantly challenged because of his French status.

At the time of Servetus' trial, it is best to think of him as an employee of the state who had temporary residency as a refugee.[1] Recognizing this, Calvin often referred to himself as a *hospes*, or a temporary guest needing shelter.[2] Calvin would be awarded bourgeois status only in 1559, six years after the trial of Servetus, and five years before his death.

The various facets of government (*Seigneurie*) are also an important element in understanding Calvin's power in Geneva. In 1553, there were three major governmental bodies: the Small Council [*Petit Conseil* or *Messieurs de Genève*],[3] the Council of Two Hundred [*Deux Cents*], and the General Assembly [*Conseil Général*].[4]

The Small Council was the most important institution in Geneva and consisted of twenty-five members. These twenty-five included the four city syndics (government officials), the treasurer, and two secretaries.[5] These *Messieurs de Genève* were native-born citizens of Geneva who bought the right of *bourgeoisie*. They met at least three times a week and had the final answer on all civil and religious matters. They had the power to hire and fire pastors, to order specific sermons for special occasions, to reprimand pastors and to punish criminals

1.   This is the message in the title of Selderhuis' book, *John Calvin: A Pilgrim's Life*.

2.   Ibid., 146.

3.   This Council is also known as *les Messieurs de Genève, Seigneurie, Senatus, Conseil Ordinaire, Conseil Estroicte*, or *Conseil*. Generally, references to the magistrates or the Genevan City Council are identical to this group.

4.   The Council of Sixty (*Conseil des Soixante*) was also another governmental body that dealt mostly with matters outside the city.

5.   See Wallace, 30; Monter, 145.

for misbehavior. By Genevan law, they controlled the trial and sentencing of Servetus.

Of lesser importance was the Council of Two Hundred. They met once a month to vote on legislation, pardon criminals (under support of the Small Council), and voted to elect members to the Small Council every February.

Finally, the General Assembly was the largest body that consisted of the heads of all major households. They met twice a year to give final consent to all new laws given by the Small Council, to elect the four syndics every January, to elect the court judge, and to fix the price of wine each November.

The relationship between Calvin the *habitant* and the magistrates of Geneva began in August 1536 when William Farel persuaded Calvin to minister in Geneva. As a French missionary, Calvin entered a volatile city in the midst of revolution and reform. A power struggle existed between Bern on the east, France on the west, and the ancient Duchy of Savoy in the middle. Following the sentiments of the patriots of Geneva (*Enfants de Genève*), the magistrates felt like the best hope for the city would be to align themselves with the Swiss Bernese. This would have religious consequences for the city.

Following the example of Zürich, Bern accepted the Reformation in the 1520s, which meant that Geneva would do likewise. The magistrates of Bern sent William Farel to Geneva as a missionary in 1532 where he enjoyed some success. By 1533 the first evangelical worship service took place and in 1534 the Catholic bishop left the city. The mass was abolished in 1535 and the Reformed faith was made law on 25 May 1536.

Following this decision, the army of Bern protected Geneva from the besieging army of the Duke of Savoy. This political maneuver promoted theological reformation, although it was not universally accepted by Geneva's Catholic majority.

It is important to note that while the city had autonomy, it was still under the political and military oversight of Bern, which enforced its reformed ideology. As E. Monter writes, 'Geneva was merely a satellite in the orbit of Bern.'[6] Consequently, this power struggle would continue to affect Genevan decisions for years to come.

Considering the foreign missionary status of Calvin, the government structure of Geneva, and the role of Bern, the following six events illustrate opposition to Calvin by the government.

1. The Lord's Supper and Calvin's Expulsion from Geneva in 1538

Although initially employed by the city as a reader in the Holy Scriptures, Calvin quickly distinguished himself and accepted a call to the pastorate. Yet, throughout his ministry in Geneva, Calvin struggled to maintain a working relationship with the magistrates. As T.H.L. Parker writes, 'In Geneva Calvin encountered bitter and prolonged opposition to his work.'[7]

The first of many bitter battles occurred during the outset of his pastoral ministry in 1537, which involved his desire to hold the Lord's Supper every week. The magistrates thought this conformed too closely with Catholic tradition, so in an attempt to compromise, Calvin suggested that it be celebrated once a month. Again, Calvin the foreigner was denied by the Council which ruled that the Supper would be celebrated four times a year (Christmas, Easter, Pentecost, and September).

Considering the religious transition that was taking place in Geneva, Calvin was concerned for the purity of the Church,

---

6. Monter, 64.
7. *John Calvin: A Biography* (Louisville KY: Westminster John Knox Press, 2006), 124.

particularly as it pertained to serving the Lord's Table to unbelievers, which also affected the matter of Church discipline. As early as 16 January 1537, Calvin and Farel submitted the 'Articles Concerning the Organization of the Church and Worship in Geneva' (*Articles concernant l'organisation de l'église et du culte à Genève*) which was concerned with instruction, discipline, and the Lord's Supper.[8] Whereas the Council was friendly to some aspects of the document, they rejected Calvin's suggestion that discipline should be administered by the Church instead of the government.

On a positive note, on 12 November 1537 the magistrates agreed with the pastors that all those who wished to stay in Geneva should give their assent to the reform. However, the *Messieurs de Genève* reneged on this decision and on 4 January 1538 insisted that Calvin was to serve Communion to everyone, even those he deemed unworthy.

As a further attack on Calvin's attempted reforms, in March 1538 Calvin and Farel were forced by the new syndics to attend a synod in Lausanne where it was decided that Geneva would follow the ecclesiastical practices of Bern. Not only were the ministers not allowed to be involved in political matters, but the *Messieurs de Berne* now dictated that Calvin was to follow their pattern of ecclesiology.[9]

Supported in this decision by the Bernese 'Articulants' (*Artichauds*) of Geneva, Calvin and Farel were restricted from ministering at Saint-Pierre Cathedral for their refusal to conform.[10] In response to the intrusion of the city into Church

---

8. This document is also known as *Articles sur le Gouvernement de l'Église*. Calvin released two other fundamental documents in this period: his *Confession of Faith* (November 1536), and *Catechism of the Church of Geneva* (November 1537).

9. *CO*, 21:222; 10b, 185–86.

10. William G. Naphy writes of Bernese interference in this matter: 'In 1538, Calvin became a victim of this foreign policy. Geneva's

affairs, Calvin and Farel protested that they would refuse communion to the entire city. Consequently, Calvin and Farel were promptly given three days to leave the city. The motto of *post tenebras lux* ('after darkness, light') had seen its dusk in Geneva with Calvin's expulsion.

2. Calvin's Return to Geneva in 1541

Following a chain of events that left Geneva in political and spiritual shambles, the magistrates implored Calvin to return to Geneva. Calvin was residing in Martin Bucer's Strasbourg and was enjoying ministry, teaching, time for writing, being a newlywed, and the fatherly discipleship of Bucer.

Although Calvin expressed his opinion that he would rather perish than return to Geneva,[11] he did write the following in his letter to Cardinal James Sadolet (1477–1547), who was seducing Geneva to return to Rome: 'Although I am for the present relieved of the charge of the church of Geneva, this circumstance ought not to prevent me from embracing it with

---

ecclesiastical system was conformed to Bern's by senatorial fiat' ('Calvin's Geneva' in *The Cambridge Companion to John Calvin*, ed. Donald K. McKim, 25–37 [Cambridge: Cambridge University Press, 2004], 28). Selderhuis concurs: 'The real issue was the debate on Geneva's level of dependence on Bern. What made things difficult for Calvin was that, at the time, political power was in the hands of the group that wanted to keep strong relations with Bern at all costs and was ready to do away with whatever might hinder those relations, including Calvin. Calvin was an easy target because, even before the Reformation, many in Geneva felt an aversion to the foreign—at that time still Catholic—clergymen they felt were trying to usurp power in the city. In short the events of 1538 were matters not of ethics or of dogmatics, but of politics' (83–84).

11. 'XLVII–To Peter Viret,' 19 May 1540, in *John Calvin: Tracts and Letters,* 4:187.

paternal affection. For God, when he charged me with it, bound me to be faithful to it for ever.'[12]

After three years, Calvin returned on 13 September 1541 an older, more mature minister, who now had more authority to exact change.[13] Despite his successes in this regard, Bruce Gordon notes, 'during the 1540s he faced strong and effective opposition as he attempted to chart a course through the choppy waters of Genevan factionalism.'[14] In part, this stemmed from Calvin's introduction of the Ecclesiastical Ordinances (*Ordonnances ecclésiastiques*) and the Consistory (*Consistoire*).

a. Ecclesiastical Ordinances

The purpose of the Ecclesiastical Ordinances was to outline the duties of the Church and the state.[15] Calvin did believe that the

---

12. 'Reply by John Calvin to Cardinal Sadolet's Letter,' in *John Calvin: Tracts and Letters*, 1:27. See also 'LIV–To Farel,' 27 October 1540, where Calvin writes, 'it is my desire that the Church of Geneva may not be left destitute; therefore, I would rather venture my life a hundred times over than betray her by my desertion' (ibid., 4:210–14).

13. Calvin famously picked up, in his verse-by-verse exposition of the Word of God, where he left off. He describes the event of his first sermon upon his return: 'When I went to preach again for the first time, there was not a soul that did not sit up straight, full of curiosity. However, I completely passed over everything that had happened and that they surely were curious to hear about, and devoted a few words to explaining the essence of my ministry. Thereafter I gave a short testimony of my faith and the sincerity of my intentions. Then I chose to expound on the passage to which I had come before my banishment. In this way I hoped to show that I had not put down my teaching office, but had only interrupted it for a while' (*CO*, 11:365–6, January 1542, quoted in Selderhuis, 118). I am indebted to Igor Gerdov for help in locating this quotation in *CO*.

14. Gordon, 124.

15. See also Calvin's comments on Deuteronomy 13:5 ('But that prophet or that dreamer of dreams shall be put to death, because he has taught rebellion against the LORD your God, who brought you out of the land of Egypt and redeemed you out of the house of slavery, to make you

Church and state were distinct entities, although they were one in purpose. Consequently, Calvin devotes a section in Chapter 4 of his *Institutes* to, 'On Civil Government.' He writes that the magistrate is a 'minister of God' who 'carries out the very judgments of God.'[16]

Consequently, Calvin agreed that the magistrates were to control matters related to punishment of criminal activity. He writes, 'For the church does not have the right of the sword to punish or compel, not the authority to force; not imprisonment, nor the other punishments which the magistrate commonly inflicts …. The church does not assume what is proper to the

---

leave the way in which the LORD your God commanded you to walk. So you shall purge the evil from your midst.'). Calvin writes, 'Capital punishment shall be decreed against adulterers; but shall the despisers of God be permitted with impunity to adulterate the doctrines of salvation, and to draw away wretched souls from the faith? Pardon shall never be extended to poisoners, by whom the body alone is injured; and shall it be sport to deliver souls to eternal destruction? Finally, the magistracy, if its own authority be assailed, shall take severe vengeance upon that contempt; and shall it suffer the profanation of God's holy name to be unavenged? What can be more monstrous! But it is superfluous to contend by argument, when God has once pronounced what is His will, for we must needs abide by His inviolable decree. But it is questioned whether the law pertains to the kingdom of Christ, which is spiritual and distinct from all earthly dominion; and there are some men, not otherwise ill-disposed, to whom it appears that our condition under the Gospel is different from that of the ancient people under the law; not only because the kingdom of Christ is not of this world, but because Christ was unwilling that the beginnings of His kingdom should be aided by the sword. But, when human judges consecrate their work to the promotion of Christ's kingdom, I deny that on that account its nature is changed' (*Calvin's Commentaries*, 22 volumes, [Grand Rapids: Baker Books, 1996], 2:76–77, vol. 2).

Of course, this does not mean that Calvin believed that Christians or ministers should slavishly follow the magistrates when they oppose the work of God. Indeed, Calvin openly preached against the actions of the magistrates when he felt it necessary (cf. *CO*, 16:43).

16. *Institutes*, 2:1497.

magistrate; nor can the magistrate execute what is carried out by the church.'[17]

The most important duty of magistrates, according to Calvin, is to 'cherish and protect the outward worship of God,' and 'to defend sound doctrine of piety and the position of the church.'[18]

While Calvin did give authority to the magistrates to elect elders in his Ordinances, the Council revised the Ordinances to give themselves more power. To the disdain of Calvin, the magistrates added the following statement to the end of the Ordinances:

> All this must be done in such a way that the ministers have no civil jurisdiction nor use anything but the spiritual sword of the word of God as St Paul commands them [cf. Rom. 13:1ff.], and that there is no derogation by this Consistory from the authority of the Seigneury or the magistracy; but the civil power shall continue in its entirety. And in cases where there is need to administer some punishment or to restrain the parties, the ministers together with the Consistory having heard the parties and administered such reprimands and admonishments as are desirable, shall report the whole matter to the Council, which thereupon shall take steps to set things in order and pass judgment according to the requirements of the case.[19]

This ruling would be a point of contention between the magistrates and Calvin for years to come, and would also have major significance for who would control the trial and execution of Servetus.

---

17. Ibid., 2:1215.
18. Ibid., 2:1487.
19. *The Register of the Company of Pastors of Geneva in the Time of Calvin*, edited and translated by Philip E. Hughes (Eugene, OR: Wipf & Stock, 1966), 49. Cf. *Institutes* 2:1215.

b. The Consistory

The second point of contention with the magistrates was the creation of the Consistory. Alister McGrath writes, 'The most distinctive and controversial aspect of Calvin's system of church government was the Consistory.'[20] This body was a general Church council that oversaw the life of the Church, particularly in matters of counseling and discipline. Although the Consistory was overbearing and intrusive by modern standards, it became the model for many reformed traditions.[21]

This body consisted of twelve lay elders who were annually selected by the magistrates, all of the Venerable Company of Pastors (less than twenty), two senators, nine members of the Council of Sixty, and one of the ruling syndics.[22] The Ordinances explain the nature of the body: 'The elders should meet once a week with the ministers, on a Thursday, to ensure that there is no disorder in the Church and to discuss together any necessary remedial action.'[23]

Contrary to popular opinion, the existence and function of the Consistory shows that Calvin was not *the* pastor of Geneva and St. Pierre Cathedral was not the only church of Geneva. There were four churches in the city: St. Gervais, St. Germain, Madeleine, and St. Pierre.[24] The pastors of these churches,

---

20. *Reformation Thought: An Introduction*, 3rd edition (Malden, MA: Blackwell Publishers, 1999), 211.

21. Robert Kingdon writes, 'That [austere] lifestyle was something that attracted many people to Calvinism throughout Europe and even in North America. In England and its colonies this style of life came to be labeled 'Puritan.' In many countries, institutions similar to the Consistory were established to promote this lifestyle, but they were not always called consistories' (Robert M. Kingdon, 'Consistory,' in *The Oxford Encyclopedia of the Reformation*), 1:417.

22. Naphy, *Calvin and the Consolidation of the Genevan Reformation*, 76.

23. *The Register of the Company of Pastors*, 47.

24. Parker writes, '… Saint Gervais and la Madeleine having their existing boundaries and St. Pierre, a new parish, embracing what had formerly

together with village churches surrounding Geneva, comprised the above-mentioned Venerable Company of Pastors, which met weekly.

A single pastor did not rule this Council, which was contrary to the traditional monarchical model of Church government that was led by a single bishop. However, Calvin was the moderator (*primus inter pares*) of this group. He understood the dangers of placing all power into the hands of one minister and wrote against this practice in his *Institutes*: 'This power ... was not in one man's possession to do whatever he pleased but in the hands of the assembly of the elders, which was to the church what the Senate is to the city.'[25]

A practical example of this concerns a disciplinary case concerning several distinguished members of Geneva. Calvin wrote to Farel, 'When the senate had asked my opinion, I said that I would make no reply unless concerning the common resolution of the brethren.'[26] In the case of Jean Ferron, Calvin excused himself from the Company so that they could give a fair assessment on whether or not he had exceeded his authority as the moderator. The Company ruled in Calvin's favor.[27]

Concerning the extent of Calvin's powers among the pastors, Kingdon writes that Calvin 'called the meetings, presided over them, announced decisions, and negotiated on behalf of

---

been Saint Germain, Saint Cross, Notre Dame-la-Neuve, and Saint Legier' (109).

25. *Institutes*, 2:1217–8. He also wrote to Melanchthon: 'In the Church we must always be on our guard lest we pay too great a deference to men. For it is all over with her, when a single individual, be he whoever you please, has more authority than all the rest, especially where this very person does not scruple to try how far he may go' ('CXXXVI–To Melanchthon,' 28 June 1545, in *John Calvin: Tracts and Letters*, 4:467). Cf. Calvin's notes on John 3:29, in *Calvin's Commentaries*, 17:134.

26. 'CLXVIII–To Farel,' 4 July 1546, in *John Calvin: Tracts and Letters*, 5:61. Cf. 'CCCII–To Farel,' 26 October 1552, ibid., 5:372.

27. See Manitsch, 63.

the company with external authorities, most commonly the governing council of Geneva .... This was his only position of pre-eminence, but he constantly deprecated it, always claiming to speak for the company as a whole and indignantly denying accusations that he was behaving like a new bishop.'[28]

Despite the ecclesial nature of this Company, 'Each minister served at the government's pleasure and could be dismissed without notice if he irritated the government through imprudent preaching or unseemly behavior.'[29] As an illustration of the limited power of this group, many of the pastors were brought before the magistrates to be reprimanded for questionable behavior (usually the content of their preaching), even Calvin himself.[30]

---

28. Robert M. Kingdon, 'Compagnie des Pasteurs,' in *The Oxford Encyclopedia of the Reformation*, 1:393. Not only does Calvin's civil status in Geneva run contrary to the typical portrayal of him as attempting to control all aspects of Genevan life, his attitude also supports the contrary opinion. For example, when an assistant teacher was needed for the College of Geneva, Calvin writes to Viret, 'With regard to the assistant-teacher, I do not venture upon anything, because it will be more satisfactory that the person who has the superintendence of the school shall have the unfettered power of selecting whom he chooses' ('CXLIX–To Viret,' 24 October 1545, in *John Calvin: Tracts and Letters*), 5:24. Cf. Calvin's commentary on Ephesians 4:11 where he decries 'tyrannical hierarchy' and describes pastors as being 'on an equal level with each other' (*Calvin's Commentaries*, 21:280–1; cf. *Institutes*, 2:1158–59).

29. Robert M. Kingdon, 'Compagnie des Pasteurs,' in *The Oxford Encyclopedia of the Reformation*, 1:393.

30. For example, Calvin was warned about his preaching on 21 May 1548, 10 July 1548 and 28 February 1552 (see Naphy, *Calvin and the Consolidation of the Genevan Reformation*, 105 [the date is incorrectly listed as 1547 on page 105, but is corrected in the reference on page 119] and 151). Bern also involved itself in these matters, even censuring Calvin's sermons. See Calvin, *Institutes*, 2:926, fn. 14 for Bern's call for Calvin to cease preaching about predestination (found in *CO*, 8:237–42).

3. The Opposition: Ami Perrin

Some prominent residents of Geneva, such as Ami Perrin (1500–1561), resented the pastors' threat of excommunication for what they considered to be minor offenses. This became a significant debate in 1545 when the Perrinists (those who supported Ami Perrin) rose in revolt to challenge the Consistory.

Although the families opposing Calvin were of high rank, Calvin was resolved to maintain impartiality in his judgments. He writes to Perrin, 'You yourself either know, or at least ought to know, what I am; that, at all events, I am one to whom the law of my heavenly Master is so dear, that the cause of no man on earth will induce me to flinch from maintaining it with a pure conscience.'[31] As was typical of Calvin, he was plain spoken to the best of his friends concerning their insufficiencies,[32] but with brotherly concern, as he did with Perrin: 'May the Lord protect you by his own defense, and discover to you how greatly even the stripes of a sincere friend are to be preferred to the treacherous blandishments of others!'[33]

Despite Calvin's efforts to reform the Perrinist party, the city council continued to be negatively influenced by them. In 1546 Calvin expressed his frustration with the city council when he wrote, 'the whole council is in a state of groundless

---

31. 'CLXIV–To Ami Perrin,' April 1546, in *John Calvin: Tracts and Letters*, 5:56–57.

32. For example, Calvin writes to his good friend, Farel, 'we only desire earnestly that, in so far as your duty will admit, you will accommodate yourself more to the people .... by fairness and moderation .... you sin to this extent .... You are aware how much we love, how much we revere you. This very affection, yea truly, this respect impels us to a more exact and strict censoriousness, because we desire earnestly that in those remarkable endowments which the Lord has conferred upon you, no spot or blemish may be found for the malevolent to find fault with, or even to carp at' ('LXXVI–To Farel,' 16 September 1541 ibid., 4:285.

33. Ibid., 5:58.

agitation. I see no one of the whole number in whom I can put confidence. I certainly observe no one here who can be said to be judicious.'[34] Agitation grew against Calvin, even to the point of an anonymous letter being placed on Calvin's pulpit, threatening him with death unless he remained silent.[35] In fact, rumors of Calvin's injury or murder were commonplace.[36]

The situation degenerated to such an extent that by 1547 Calvin believed it likely that he would once again be expelled from Geneva. He confided to Farel, 'Affairs are certainly in such a state of confusion that I despair of being able longer to retain this church, at least by my own endeavors.'[37] He also wrote to his close confidant Pierre Viret (1511–1571) concerning the power of his opponents in the city leadership: 'I hardly hope to be able any longer to retain any kind of position for the Church, especially under my ministry. My influence is gone, believe me, unless God stretch forth his hand.'[38]

To the dismay of Calvin, the Perrinists gained control of the government in 1548, which led to the eventual election of Perrin as mayor in 1549.[39] Out of the four new syndics elected in 1552, the year prior to the execution of Servetus in Geneva, three were relatives or supporters of Ami Perrin.

The mood of the council then moved from opposition, to provocation. On one occasion, a prospective deacon was

---

34. 'CXC–To Viret,' 27 March 1547, in *John Calvin: Tracts and Letters*, 5:106. Cf. 'XCXIII–To Francis Dryander,' 18 May 1547, ibid., 5:111–12.

35. 'CXCIX–To Viret,' 2 July 1547, ibid., 5:122–23.

36. 'CC–To Monsieur de Falais,' 14 July 1547, ibid., 5:127; 'CCIII–To Monsieur de Falais,' 16 August 1547, ibid., 5:134; 'CCIV–To Farel,' 21 August 1547, ibid., 5:137. See footnote 2 for the rumor that Calvin's opponents were willing to give five hundred crowns to have him put to death.

37. 'CCX–To Farel,' 14 December 1547, ibid., 5:147–48.

38. 'CCXI–To Viret,' 14 December 1547, ibid., 5:149.

39. By 1553 Perrin was the first syndic of Geneva (Wendel, 93).

denied the position by the magistrates because of what Calvin understood as 'no other reason than that he was for some time my coadjutor.'[40] In September of 1548 Calvin wrote to Viret, 'it be the stratagem of the ungodly to afford them a weapon for the purpose of injuring me, as often as it shall be advantageous for them to employ it …. they omit no wickedness by which they may overthrow me.'[41] At this time Calvin was summoned to the magistracy to account for his critical attitude towards them, which confirmed Calvin's fear that he would soon be forced to leave the city.[42]

4. French Refugees

Another issue that exacerbated the opposition to Calvin was the influx of refugees to Geneva in the 1540s.[43] By 1546, French ministers such as Nicolas des Gallars, Raymond Chauvet, François Bourgoing and Michel Cop were leading French figures in Geneva. The magistrates allowed foreigners to purchase bourgeois status in order to bring revenue to the city, but the separation of French and Genevan communities caused further division and distrust, as well as rising prices in the city. It is important to remember that Calvin was French, which drew unwanted attention to himself as a sojourner.

An example of Genevan xenophobia is the prayer of Louis Bandière in 1550: 'God take the preachers. They have consumed

---

40. 'CCLIV–To John Haller,' 26 November 1549, in *John Calvin: Tracts and Letters*, 5:250.

41. 'CCXXVII–To Viret,' 20 September 1548, ibid., 5:178. Cf. 'CCLXXIII–To Viret,' 24 January 1551, ibid., 5:298.

42. *CO*, 21:434–41.

43. Herman J. Selderhuis writes, 'Between October 1538 and October 1539 a total of 10,657 refugees were given aid as they passed through Geneva; during the same period the entire population of the city was about 12,000 residents' (147).

their goods and lands in France and want to take over here.' He added, 'the foreigners want to rule over us,' and 'the devil can take all foreigners, they can go and eat their God of paste elsewhere [referring to Calvin's view of the Lord's Supper].[44] Claude Tapponier even suggested that all the French people in Geneva should be burned.[45] In addition to the citizens of Geneva, Bern looked upon the influx of people from France as a threat to their control of the city, and with rumors of war, the foreigners were looked upon with suspicion.[46]

Another French refugee that caused commotion in the city was Jérôme Bolsec (d. 1584). In 1551 he publicly challenged the doctrine of predestination as 'making an idol of God.'[47] The magistrates arrested Bolsec for this, but they could not decide how to handle the case. In order to assert their own authority, the magistrates bypassed the pastors of Geneva and wrote to three Swiss cities to ask their opinion.[48] Of significance, Calvin complained to Farel, 'The Senate did not consider the pastors

---

44. Quoted in William G. Naphy, 'Baptisms, Church Riots and Social Unrest in Calvin's Geneva,' *Sixteenth Century Journal*, 26 (1995), 93. See also Naphy, *Calvin and the Consolidation of the Genevan Reformation*, 150.

45. Naphy, 215.

46. Parker writes, 'When in February 1538 a French agent actually did pay a secret visit to the city and later make overtures for a French alliance through two of the leading supporters of the Reformers, suspicion seemed confirmed. Mobs demonstrated outside their houses at night, firing off guns and threatening to chuck them into the river. Thus, to oppose Calvin became an act of patriotism' (T.H.L. Parker, *John Calvin: A Biography* [Louisville KY: Westminster John Knox Press, 2006], 89). See *CO*, 9:892.

47. 'CCLXXXIV–To Bullinger,' 15 October 1551, in *John Calvin: Tracts and Letters*, 5:319–22; 'CCLXXXV–To the Ministers of Switzerland,' October 1551, ibid., 5:322–25.

48. This issue was to rise again in 1552 when Jean Trolliet expressed his displeasure at the doctrine, but after hearing the opinions of the other Swiss cities on the Bolsec affair, and following the reading of Calvin's *Institutes*, the city supported Calvin's understanding of predestination.

worthy of being written to, but to heighten the insult, they limited their communication to the Magistrates.[49] Calvin was so dismayed that he told the Council that he would rather be discharged from his office than suffer so much in it.[50]

On 24 July 1552 Calvin was accosted by opponents, which led to his request to resign. In a candid picture of the situation, the city record reads, 'M. Calvin has remonstrated and asked that the council will not be displeased if, since he sees that some wish him ill, and many grumble and turn away from the Word, he goes into retirement and serves no longer.'[51] Despite this request, Calvin was denied by the magistrates. As Parker writes, 'The Libertines [wanted] a Calvin subservient, not a Calvin martyred by banishment and opposing them from Basel or Zürich.'[52]

As a window into the debilitating nature of the situation, in January of 1553 Calvin laments that he could not attend a friend's wedding because of the threat of being

> detained at home by the wickedness of those who cease not to bring destruction upon themselves and the community by their madness. I have good reason to call it madness, for they have never exhibited more unbridled licentiousness. I shall say nothing of their mischievous plots for the destruction of the faith, of their gross contempt of God, of their impious conspiracies for the scattering of the Church, of the foul Epicurism of their whole life …. The entire Republic is at present in disorder, and they are striving to root up the established order of things …. I cannot move a foot at present.

---

49. 'CCLXXXVIII–To Farel,' 8 December 1551, in *John Calvin: Tracts and Letters*, 5:329.

50. *CO*, 21:516.

51. Ibid., 21:547 quoted in Parker, *John Calvin: A Biography*, 145.

52. Ibid.

I have not been through the city-gates for a month past, not even for recreation.[53]

Thus was the power of Calvin in the year that Servetus entered Geneva.

5. The Lord's Supper Revisited

The question of to whom the pastors were allowed to serve Communion was a significant debate in 1553. Since the Table was only offered four times a year (Christmas, Easter, Pentecost, and September), Easter 1553 gave the Perrinist Council an opportunity to exert its authority over the pastors.

Prior to Easter, the magistrates asked the Consistory to provide it with the names of all those excommunicated and disallowed from the Table. The ministers understood the message that was being sent to the Consistory: the magistrates have the power to dictate who is excommunicated and who can partake of the Table. The pastors naturally objected.

In response, the Council ruled that ministers, even if citizens, were not to be allowed to sit on the General Council. This is the body that elected the ruling syndics, so the influence of the ministers in general, and Calvin in particular, were further limited. To make things worse, the Council unilaterally moved the minister of the nearby village of Jussy to Geneva and replaced him with their candidate without the consultation of the pastors.

---

53. 'CCCVIII–To Christopher Fabri,' 13 January 1553, in *John Calvin: Tracts and Letters*, 5:387–88.

6. The Philibert Berthelier Affair

As illustrated above, part of the ongoing tension between the magistrates and the Company of Pastors involved who had the authority to ban someone from partaking of the Lord's Supper. Going back to March of 1543 the Council of Sixty recommended that the Consistory have no jurisdiction in this matter.[54] The Council judged, 'the Consistory should have neither jurisdiction nor power to ban from the supper, but only to admonish and then to report to the Council, so that the Seigneury might pass judgment on the delinquents according to their deserts.' Since this issue was an important element in his initial banishment from Geneva in 1538, Calvin vehemently defended the right of the pastors' conscience in serving the Supper.[55] This was again reinforced in favor of the pastors in *The Registry of the Company of Pastors* in 1541.[56]

Although the magistrates finally compromised in order to have peace with the pastors, the issue was raised again in 1548 when the Council ordered the pastors to give the sacrament to a man named Amar and to Guichard Roux on the basis that the Consistory only had the right 'of admonition and not of excommunication.'[57] This power struggle would again be raised during Servetus' trial.

When things were uncertain as to Servetus' fate, and in the midst of the debate concerning who had more power to judge him, the situation was exacerbated by an old excommunication

---

54. *The Register of the Company of Pastors*, 11.
55. Cf. 'CII–To Viret,' the day before Easter 1543, in *John Calvin: Tracts and Letters*, 4:377.
56. 'The Order to be Maintained in the Case of Adults for Preserving Discipline in the Church,' 47–49.
57. Ibid., 11. The Genevan catechism of 1537 expressly states that excommunication is the prerogative of the church ('Catechism of the Church of Geneva', in *John Calvin: Tracts and Letters*), 2:94.

case that would pit Calvin against the magistrates. Two years prior, Philibert Berthelier, the son of a Genevan patriot, was arrested in October 1552 and excommunicated for insulting and mocking Genevan pastor, Raymond Chauvet.[58] As a significant affront to the pastors of Geneva, three days after Berthelier was released from jail, and while he was still under excommunication, Berthelier was elected to be an assistant to the Lieutenant of the city in November of 1552, which means he would play a significant leadership role in the trial of Servetus.

Recognizing the appearance of things, the magistrates ordered that the pastors be reconciled with Berthelier so that he could partake of Communion at Christmas. Once summoned before the pastors, Berthelier 'showed the same or even greater rebelliousness than before,' and thus, on the recommendation of the pastors and the magistrates, Berthelier was not permitted to take Communion.[59] Infuriated, Berthelier continued to slander the pastors and was reprimanded again in February 1553 for stating that pastor Jean Louis Favre was 'a wicked man.'[60]

On 1 September 1553, two weeks after Servetus' arrest, while the Council was waiting for the reply of the Swiss cities concerning the fate of Servetus, Berthelier bypassed the Consistory and directly appealed to the Little Council to take the Supper in September.[61] As a result, in the manner of 1538

---

58. Naphy, *Calvin and the Consolidation of the Genevan Reformation*, 151–52. Berthelier had previous encounters with the law when he was reprimanded for interrupting Calvin's preaching with intentional loud coughing (1547), drunkenness and assault (1548), and having an affair (1551) (see Parker, 126 and Wallace, 61). To understand the character of Berthelier, when he was confronted for interrupting Calvin with coughing, he replied that he could produce more bodily noises that would be more irritating (Selderhuis, 114).

59. *The Register of the Company of Pastors*, 204–05.

60. Naphy, *Calvin and the Consolidation of the Genevan Reformation,* 180.

61. *The Register of the Company of Pastors,* 285–86. Although it cannot be proven, Ronald Wallace suggests that Berthelier did this strategically

when Calvin was expelled from Geneva, Calvin informed the Council that he would refuse to serve the Lord's Supper to Berthelier under pain of his own life. Although the Council publicly upheld their position against Calvin, they privately told Berthelier to abstain from the Table in order to avoid controversy.

The next day, Sunday, 3 September 1553, was one of the most defining moments of Calvin's ministry in Geneva. As Kayayan notes, 'The fate of Calvin and of the Reformation was thus at stake on that Sunday morning … in the church of St. Pierre.'[62] Not knowing that the Small Council had advised Berthelier not to partake of the Lord's Supper, Calvin proclaimed, 'Since we now are going to receive the Supper of our Lord Jesus Christ, if anyone tries to intrude on this table, though he has been defended by the Consistory to do so, it is certain that at the cost of my life I will prove to be what I am commanded to be.'[63] Risking everything, Calvin's life and legacy came down to this one moment. Berthelier remained seated.

Significantly, that afternoon Calvin preached on Acts 20 where Paul gives his farewell address to the Ephesian elders.[64] Believing that the prejudice against him during the trial of Servetus would provoke the end of his ministry in Geneva, Calvin concluded his sermon by saying, 'Since these things are so, allow me also, brethren, to use these words of the Apostle, "I commend you to the Lord, and to the Word of His grace."'[65]

It is important to remember that Calvin would have given this 'farewell sermon' during Servetus' trial in response to his

---

at the behest of Calvin's opponent, Ami Perrin (*Calvin, Geneva and the Reformation*, 61).

62. 'The Case of Michael Servetus,' 136.

63. Quoted in ibid., 136–37.

64. Beza, 'The Life of John Calvin,' 1:lxiii.

65. Ibid.

utter lack of influence upon the city. As Naphy notes, 'The threat to ministerial power posed by Berthelier's appeal … in Calvin's view, had the potential to end his ministry in Geneva, if not his life as well.'[66] In that regard, Calvin writes to Viret:

> The reply was, that the Senate had nothing to change in its former decision [to give such power to the pastors]. From which you perceive, that by this law my ministry is abandoned, if I suffer the authority of the Consistory to be trampled upon, and extend the Supper of Christ to open scoffers, who boast that pastors are nothing to them. In truth, I should rather die a hundred times, than subject Christ to such foul mockery …. But if God yields so much power to Satan, as to strip me of the liberty of my ministry by his violent commands, I am satisfied. Certainly, he who has inflicted the wound, will himself find a remedy. And, indeed, seeing that so much wickedness has now passed with impunity for many years, perhaps the Lord is preparing some judgment which I am not deemed worthy to see.[67]

Realizing that Calvin's ministry was in serious jeopardy, on 7 September the other pastors of Geneva sent letters to the other Swiss reformed cities and took a mutual pact to resign *en masse* if the magistrates continued on their course.

On 18 September, the Small Council expressed that they were sympathetic to the pastors' concern, but overruled the Consistory's decision by offering a compromise that allowed for Berthelier to take Communion after a period of time. This would have averted the mass resignation of the pastors, while preserving the right of the magistrates to decide such cases.

---

66. Naphy, *Calvin and the Consolidation of the Genevan Reformation,* 183.
67. 'CCCXXV–To Viret,' 4 September 1553, in *John Calvin: Tracts and Letters,* 5:425.

Calvin was once again defeated.[68] This decision was reaffirmed in November when it was established that 'the final word will be with the council.'[69]

It is vital to understand that the majority of the Genevan council during the trial of Servetus consisted of the enemies of Calvin, known as the 'Libertines.' Even during the trial of Servetus, Calvin believed that the Perrinists in general, and Berthelier in particular, were attempting to aid Servetus.[70] For example, on 15 September, Servetus made a written appeal to make his case before the Council of Two Hundred. Realizing that Servetus should not have known about the inner-workings of Genevan politics, many historians have posited that Servetus must have made this request at the instigation of Perrin and Berthelier. As Gordon writes, 'This was part of an orchestrated move to limit the authority of the ministers in the city that included plans to prohibit them from speaking in the General Council. At the same time, the Perrinist party sought to clip the political wings of Calvin's supporters by excluding many of

---

68. This divisiveness would continue until the defeat of the Perrinist party in 1555, which eventually saw the Small Council populated by a majority of Calvin's supporters. The fragile nature of this victory is noted by Gordon: 'Victory in Geneva was never a foregone conclusion. Had the Perrinist party not lost control of the situation through its own blunders and internal rancorousness, Calvin might have been dislodged during the debates over church discipline. Certainly the Frenchman was at times despondent about his chances. Opposition in the city was considerable and well connected with outside powers' (216).

69. *CO*, 21:560. This debate would continue through 1554 when Calvin was still unsure of his future in Geneva. Parker writes, 'When 1554 came Calvin was still thinking he would have to leave' (155). This is affirmed by Calvin's letter to Farel: 'Here at home everything is in fearful confusion .... On the inner discords of our city I am afraid that you will soon be getting bad news' (*CO*, 15, 617–18).

70. 'CCCXXXV–To the Pastors and Doctors of the Church of Zürich,' 26 November 1553, in *John Calvin: Tracts and Letters*, 5:443.

them from elections.'[71] Again, the goal was not to evict Calvin from Geneva, but to embarrass him and limit his authority. In the words of Parker, 'It would be better for the Philistines if Samson remained in Gaza, his locks shorn.'[72]

Parker also affirms that Calvin was debased at this time: 'It was at this point, when Calvin's authority in Geneva was at its lowest, when he was in fact defeated ...'[73] In a letter to Bullinger of Zürich, Calvin expressed his personal difficulty with the magistrates: 'Indeed they cause you this trouble despite our admonitions, but they have reached such a state of folly and madness that they regard with suspicion whatever we say to them. So much so, that were I to allege that it is clear at mid-day they would immediately begin to doubt it!'[74] Furthermore, he writes, 'Here in the republic there is such chaos that the church is being tossed back and forth by God as Noah's ark was by the waves of the flood,' and 'they try to test my patience by provoking me often and in many ways.'[75] Alister McGrath concurs with this conclusion: 'The Perrinists had recently gained power, and were determined to weaken his position. Their prosecution of Servetus ... was intended to demonstrate their impeccable orthodoxy, as a prelude to undermining Calvin's religious authority within the city. The Consistory—the normal instrument of ecclesiastical discipline, over which Calvin had considerable influence—was bypassed altogether by the council in its efforts to marginalize Calvin from the affair.'[76]

---

71. Gordon, 212. Cf. Kayan, 137.
72. Parker, 139.
73. Ibid., 146.
74. 'CCCXXVI–To Bullinger,' 7 September 1553, in *John Calvin: Tracts and Letters*, 5:427.
75. Selderhuis, 206.
76. *A Life of John Calvin*, (Cambridge, MA: Blackwell Publishers, 1995), 116. Schaff writes, 'We do not know whether Servetus was aware of this

It was in this hopeless season, when Calvin despaired of his ministry and even his life, that Servetus entered Geneva.[77]

---

state of things. But he could not have come at a time more favorable to him and more unfavorable to Calvin. Among the Libertines and Patriots, who hated the yoke of Calvin even more than the yoke of the pope, Servetus found natural supporters who, in turn, would gladly use him for political purposes. This fact emboldened him to take such a defiant attitude in the trial and to overwhelm Calvin with abuse' (*History of the Christian Church*, 8:767. Cf. ibid., 8:781).

77. No doubt Calvin expected martyrdom to be his own end: 'But let us now live so for Christ, that we may be daily prepared to die for him; we ought, while we have opportunity, to prepare for what will befall us' ('CCCXII–To Farel,' 27 March 1553, in *John Calvin: Tracts and Letters*, 5:396). Beza also writes of the critical nature of the situation: 'The following year, viz., 1553, while the malice of the factious, which was hastening to its close, was so boisterous, that not only the Church, but even the Republic itself, was brought into extreme jeopardy .... it seemed nothing could prevent [the Libertines] from accomplishing the design for which they had long agitated, as they had everything in their power' ('The Life of John Calvin,' 1:lx–lxi).

4

SERVETUS' ARREST, TRIAL AND EXECUTION IN GENEVA

Servetus had been on the run since his escape from the Viennese prison, but resolved to flee to Naples, Italy to practice medicine. In a decision that was a mystery to Calvin, and remains a mystery to this day, Servetus took a detour through Geneva and attended a Sunday afternoon church service on 13 August 1553.[1]

At his trial, Servetus claimed that he stopped by the city for one night with the hope of remaining hidden. However, this testimony is unconvincing because Geneva was not on the way to Naples. Taking into account the unrest in Geneva, particularly as it pertains to opposition to Calvin, the words of Wolfgang Musculus (1497–1563; the minister of Bern) are of particular interest: 'Servetus had recently come to Geneva

---

1. *CO*, 14:589.

to take advantage of the rancor with which the government pursued Calvin. He hoped to obtain a foothold from which he would be able to carry on the affair with the other churches.'[2] There is also evidence that Servetus had been in Geneva for a few weeks prior to his arrest in order to foment a *coup d'état* with the Libertines, although this is doubtful.[3]

While the coup option cannot be proven, Gordon gives a more likely possibility for Servetus' visit to Geneva:

> It was not a mistake. Servetus' repeated attempts to make contact with Calvin bordered on obsession. His arrival in Geneva was a provocation shaped by an apocalyptic view that in the final days as the Four Horsemen rode across Europe he would confront the man he held responsible for turning the Reformation into a new Rome. Servetus had arrived to make his final stand. In Geneva he would give a full account of his views, and die a martyr. There would be no more flight or hiding—it was time to face his persecutors, and his most hated enemy.[4]

Although Servetus could have been motivated by such fateful romanticism, it seems more plausible to suggest that, as in his previous forays into Basel and Strasbourg, Servetus was hopeful to convince *the* leader of the Reformation that his doctrine was true. If he could accomplish that, then he could restore Christianity to its original moorings. Other than such motivations to visit Geneva, it could have been that Servetus simply came to see one of her greatest tourist attractions—John Calvin.

---

2.   Ibid., 14:628.
3.   Ibid., 14:590, fn. 1. Roland Bainton argues against this hypothesis in his article, 'Servetus and the Genevan Libertines.'
4.   Gordon, 219.

Servetus was recognized after the Sunday sermon in Madeleine church on 13 August. Knowing that Servetus had been arrested in Vienne for heresy, Calvin reported Servetus to the authorities.[5] The sixty-three page account of the arrest, trial and execution of Servetus in *The Register of the Company of Pastors* explains how things began:

> On 13 August of this year Michael Servetus was recognized by certain brethren and it was decided that he should be imprisoned lest he should further infect the world with his blasphemies and heresies, seeing that he was known to be altogether beyond hope of correction. Thereupon, a certain person [Nicolas de la Fontaine, Calvin's secretary] had filed a criminal action against him, setting down ... the most notorious errors of Servetus. Several days later the Council ordered that we should be present when he was examined. When this was done the impudence and obstinacy of Servetus became all the more obvious; for, to begin with, he maintained

---

5. 'CCCXXII–To Farel,' 20 August 1553, in *John Calvin: Tracts and Letters*, 5:417. It has been suggested that Calvin should have let Servetus pass through the city, but not only did Calvin not know the motive of Servetus for being in Geneva, his entertainment of Servetus would have been in violation of the law, and would certainly have been used by the libertarians to further attack Calvin. This is not only for theological heresy, but for Anabaptist views that were understood to be revolutionary, seditious, and a threat to the peace of Geneva.

    For his part, Calvin justifies his actions based upon the health of the Church. He writes that Servetus escaped from prison 'some way or other, and wandered in Italy for nearly four months. At length, in an evil hour, he came to this place, when, at my instigation, one of the syndics ordered him to be conducted to prison; for I do not disguise it that I considered it my duty to put a check, so far as I could, upon this most obstinate and ungovernable man, that his contagion might not spread farther. We see with what wantonness impiety is making progress everywhere, so that new errors are ever and anon breaking forth; we see how very inactive those are whom God has armed with the sword for the vindication of the glory of his name' ('CCCXXVII–To Sulzer,' 8 September 1553, in *John Calvin: Tracts and Letters*, 5:428).

that the name of the Trinity had been in use only since the Council of Nicea [325] and that all the theologians and martyrs prior to that had not known what it was. And when the plainest evidences were produced from Justin Martyr, Irenaeus, Tertullian, Origen, and others, so far was he from showing any shame that he poured out all sorts of absurdities in a most insulting and offensive manner.[6]

Upon Servetus' arrest, the Magistracy took over the case according to the instruction of the Ecclesiastical Ordinances of 1541. The court likely used the Genevan 1542 Edict of the Lieutenant, the 1543 Ordinances on Offices and Officers, and Imperial law as a basis for its proceedings and judgments. Since the pastors could only recommend cases of excommunication, the trial of Servetus was entirely a secular affair.[7] Consequently, Servetus never appeared before the Company of Pastors or the Consistory.

The city Lieutenant, Pierre Tissot investigated the case and eventually gave the case to his assistant, Philibert Berthelier (excommunicated at the time), who would be assisted by the syndic, Ami Perrin (Calvin's leading critic).[8] The prosecutor would be Claude Rigot, also a supporter of Ami Perrin.

---

6. *The Register of the Company of Pastors*, 223–4. See also *CO*, 8:725.

7. Despite the fact that Calvin did not judge Servetus, there has always been the charge that Calvin personally condemned and executed him. Calvin's letter to Bullinger after the death of Servetus is particularly concerning: 'there are others who assail me harshly as a master in cruelty and atrocity, for attacking with my pen not only a dead man, but one who perished by my hands ... But it is well that I have you for the partner of my fault, if fault indeed there is, since you were my prompter and exhorter' ('CCCXLVIII–To Bullinger,' 28 April 1554, in *John Calvin: Tracts and Letters*, 6:36). Considering the overall context, it is likely that Calvin is admitting to taking part in the condemnation of Servetus through his testimony by drawing up of the thirty-eight articles against Servetus' doctrine. As will be shown, legally he could not condemn or put anyone to death.

8. Parker, 151.

Considering the relationship between the magistrates and Calvin, the Council seemed resolved not to allow Calvin to decide the fate of Servetus. Consequently, the trial was marred by the political struggle in Geneva.[9]

The first hearing before the court took place on 14 August, and prosecutor Claude Rigot denied Servetus the opportunity to have legal counsel according to the city ordinances of 1543, which allowed for such a scenario.[10] From the beginning, Servetus was intent upon publicly insulting Calvin. 'He impudently reviled me,' writes Calvin, 'just as if he regarded me as obnoxious to him.'[11]

On 17 August the magistrates did make use of Calvin by requesting that he draw up theological accusations. Calvin produced thirty-eight articles against Servetus and was called to be a witness against him.[12] Servetus was then allowed to prepare a defense, for which Calvin gave him books from his personal library for research.[13]

When testimony began, the minutes were recorded in *The Register of the Company of Pastors*.[14] Calvin's thirty-eight articles were debated one-by-one with the Ministers making a claim, and Servetus responding. Following this debate, Servetus was recommended to the attorney-general, Claude Rigot, who initiated the criminal phase of the trial. He submitted thirty articles which dealt primarily with the danger of Servetus and his doctrine to Christian society.[15] Servetus defended himself

---

9. Details of the trial can be found in *CO*, 8:725–872.

10. For Rigot's opinion of Servetus, see *CO*, 8:774.

11. 'CCCXXII–To Farel,' 20 August 1553, in *John Calvin: Tracts and Letters*, 5:417.

12. These may be found in *The Register of the Company of Pastors*.

13. *CO*, 8:480.

14. See pages 224–84.

15. *CO*, 8:763–66.

against these charges on 24 August and Rigot then responded to Servetus, appealing to Church tradition for the execution of heretics.

A significant factor to consider is how Servetus conducted himself during the trial. Reminiscent of how he wrote to Œcolampadius, the treatment he gave his professors in Paris, and his method of corresponding with Calvin and Poupin, Servetus once again distinguished himself by his insults and sarcasm. Although it must be stated that the Ministers could be harsh with their language against Servetus, it is striking to observe the behavior of Servetus before those whom he knew held his life in their hands.

Servetus mocked and cast aspersions upon the Ministers in general and Calvin in particular. Over twenty-five times in the notes of the trial, Servetus likened Calvin to the father of all heresies, the sorcerer Simon Magus.[16] Other language includes (but is not limited to) the following toward Calvin or the pastors: '[you have] Cain-like faith, homicidal';[17] 'you are a worthless and shameless twister';[18] 'O blindest wretch!';[19] 'You are a Simon Magus, always wicked and perverse';[20] 'You ridiculous mouse,'[21] 'wisdom cannot enter your malevolent mind';[22] 'Most worthless wretch';[23] 'you are completely ignorant';[24] 'All is well, except that you have a perverted mind';[25] 'You are lower than

---

16. Ibid., 8:514, 535–36.
17. *The Register of the Company of Pastors*, 226.
18. Ibid., 229.
19. Ibid., 233.
20. Ibid.
21. Ibid., 240.
22. Ibid., 257.
23. Ibid., 268.
24. Ibid., 272.
25. Ibid., 274.

the lowest';[26] 'it is in Satan that you move';[27] and 'you worthless wretch.'[28]

In response to one charge by Calvin, Servetus replied, 'The objection is so stupid that if Calvin had a grain of intelligence he would be ashamed to repeat it so often …. wretched man …. clumsy slanderer.'[29] In another specific reference to Calvin, Servetus said, 'one cannot help being amazed at the shamelessness of this man, who declares himself to be orthodox when he is a disciple of Simon Magus …. Who would call a criminal accuser and a murderer an orthodox minister of the Church?' He goes on to say, 'Truly so, and a follower of Simon Magus. Deny that you are a murderer and I will prove it by deeds. You dare not deny that you are a Simon Magus. Who, then, may trust you and believe that you are a good tree? In so just a case I stand firm and do not fear death.'[30]

The records of Geneva give special attention to Servetus' behavior in their account of the trial. In typical fashion that has caused some scholars to question his mental stability,[31] Servetus petitioned the Little Council with the following demands on 22 October: '[Calvin should] be made a prisoner like me until the matter be settled by my death or his or another penalty …. And I shall be glad to die if he be not convicted of this and other things which I mentioned below. I demand justice, my Lords, justice, justice!'[32] Servetus continued his appeal to the Council against Calvin: 'as a sorcerer he should be not only

---

26. Ibid., 277.

27. Ibid., 280.

28. Ibid., 283.

29. Ibid., 269.

30. Ibid., 253.

31. Richard C. Gamble, 'Calvin's Controversies,' in *The Cambridge Companion to John Calvin* (ed. Donald K. McKim; Cambridge: Cambridge University Press, 2004), 197.

32. *CO*, 8:805, quoted in Bainton, *Hunted Heretic*, 134.

condemned but exterminated and driven from this city and his goods should be adjudged to me in recompense for mine.'[33]

These are telling statements from a man that is championed as a hero of free-thinking and tolerance.[34] There is no doubt that the behavior of this 'thoroughly unsavory character' affected the decision of the magistrates to execute Servetus. The court minutes record the following: 'so far was he from showing any shame that he poured out all sorts of absurdities in a most insulting and offensive manner,'[35] 'Servetus has with his customary petulance and without any shame calumniously twisted what we ... have set out,'[36] 'With his customary arrogance he accuses us of barking like dogs .... But we have only discharged the duty laid upon us by the Council.'[37] Also, 'Servetus will certainly get first prize for insults!'[38] The pastors conjectured what would be: 'Were he a man of mild and docile spirit,' but lamented, 'what diabolical arrogance' he displayed.[39]

The facts of Servetus' behavior are so convincing that even universalist Standford Rives, who condemns Calvin as a blood-thirsty murderer, recognizes that 'Servetus used some very poor rhetoric.'[40] Schaff summarizes the evidence: 'Servetus had

33. Ibid., 8:804–0, quoted in Bainton, *Hunted Heretic*, 135.

34. Bainton writes, 'the idea of religious tolerance is his most enduring legacy' (*Hunted Heretic*, xxix).

35. *The Register of the Company of Pastors*, 224.

36. Ibid., 226.

37. Ibid., 262–63.

38. Ibid., 274.

39. Ibid., 281. In this regard, Samuel Taylor Coleridge writes, 'if ever a poor fanatic thrust himself into the fire, it was Michael Servetus. He was a rabid enthusiast, and did every thing he could in the way of insult and ribaldry to provoke the feeling of the Christian church' (*Specimens of the Table Talk of Samuel Taylor Coleridge*, 2nd edition [London: John Murray, 1837], 283).

40. *Did Calvin Murder Servetus?* (BookSurge Publishing, 2008), 180. This self-published book is largely based on secondary resources,

much uncommon sense, but little practical common sense. He lacked balance and soundness. There was a streak of fanaticism in his brain. His eccentric genius bordered closely on the line of insanity.' Furthermore, 'he was vain, proud, defiant, quarrelsome, revengeful, irreverent in the use of language, deceitful, and mendacious.'[41] Servetus' conduct would have qualified him to be considered an insolent, obstinate heretic, which would have caused the magistrates to be more cautious and strict with their judgment.

By 21 August, the Little Council wrote to Vienne, where Servetus was originally condemned to die, and asked for duplicates of the evidence, information on the arrest warrant, and reasons for Servetus' escape.[42] On the same day, as an open expression of no confidence in the pastors of Geneva (and against their remonstrances),[43] the Council sent letters to Zürich, Bern, Basel, and Schaffhausen to ask their opinion on what should be done with Servetus.[44] There is a range of speculation concerning Geneva's appeal to these cities, but it could have involved buying time, gaining the support of other Protestant cities as cover for their final decision, or a deliberate attempt to undermine the pastors' authority in ecclesiastical issues.

Concerning Calvin's personal opinion on Servetus' fate, he did support the death penalty, which he considered primarily

---

unitarian history, contains numerous historical errors, and should not be trusted as a scholarly resource. Writing from a similar perspective, the Goldstones acknowledge, 'He could be rude, intolerant, and domineering–unwilling and probably unable to moderate his passion or his views in order to achieve a larger goal. A less politic person is hard to imagine' (96).

41. Schaff, *History of the Christian Church*, 8:787–88.
42. *CO*, 8:761, 783, 790.
43. 'CCCXXVI–To Bullinger,' 7 September 1553, in *John Calvin: Tracts and Letters*, 5:427.
44. *CO*, 8:803.

to be based upon the Bible, and secondarily on Imperial law.[45] In one of his most cited letters on this topic, Calvin writes to Farel, 'I hope that the sentence of death will at least be passed upon him; but I desire that the severity of the punishment may be mitigated.'[46]

Calvin later called upon all honest men to witness, and challenged anyone who doubted his claim, that from the time Servetus was convicted of his heresy, that he (Calvin) did not utter a word about his punishment during the trial.[47] In an attempt to gain support for the condemnation of Servetus' doctrine, and the destruction of his books, Calvin wrote to warn the French believers in Frankfurt.[48] In the meantime, a new challenge to Calvin's authority threatened to humble him even more.

Upholders of Orthodoxy

One of the consequences of the magistrates controlling Servetus' case is that all of the pressure was put on them to uphold the orthodox theology of the Reformation. First, the magistrates were concerned to avoid the opprobrium of Libertarians by permitting heresy in their midst. Second, the leaders of the Catholic Church were waiting to see how this leading city of Protestantism would handle the case. Would Geneva uphold

---

45. Farel later rebuked Calvin for this by writing, 'In desiring to mitigate the severity of his punishment, you act the part of a friend to a man who is most hostile to you … I must be prepared to suffer death if I should teach anything contrary to the doctrine of piety. And I added, that I should be most worthy of any punishment whatever, if I should seduce any one from the faith and doctrine of Christ' (*John Calvin: Tracts and Letters*, 5:417. fn. 2; cf. *CO*, 9:71).

46. 'CCCXXII–To Farel,' ibid., 2:417.

47. *CO*, 8:461.

48. 'CCCXXIV–To His Dearly Beloved, the Pastors of the Church of Frankfort,' 5:422–23.

Imperial law as did the Catholics in Vienne, or would she aid and abet a heretic by letting him live?

As a testimony of the confused nature of the city Council, François Wendel explains:

> even before they [the other reformation cities] had replied, the act of accusation had been drawn up, and it was an adversary of Calvin who wrote it. Soon the political partisans and enemies of Calvin were outbidding one another at the expense of Servetus. In the meanwhile, the ecclesiastical tribune at Vienne demanded the extradition of the heretic, which the Magistracy refused categorically, eager to prove to the world that there were judges in Geneva who knew as well as anyone how to condemn heresy.[49]

Also making this an issue of infighting and power, McGrath writes, 'If there was one area of civic life which the city council was determined to keep totally within its control, it was the administration of justice.'[50]

In response to Geneva's letter for evidence from Vienne, the Catholics sent representatives, including the jailor and captain, who brought the copy of the sentence against Servetus. In an attempt to absolve itself of the problem, the magistrates gave Servetus a choice—return to Vienne or stay in Geneva. In a response that justifies a high view of the court proceedings in Geneva, Servetus reportedly begged with tears that he be allowed to stay in Geneva.[51]

---

49. François Wendel, *Calvin: Origins and Development of His Religious Thought,* translated by Philip Mairet, (Grand Rapids: Baker, 2002), 96.

50. *A Life of John Calvin,* 114.

51. *CO,* 8:789–90. In retrospect, this was the one opportunity that Geneva had to relieve herself of Servetus, although it apparently would have conveyed weakness for the magistrates to do so.

There is no doubt that Geneva's refusal to deliver Servetus to Vienne put further pressure on them to mete out justice since they could not be seen as being any less zealous for the truth than their detractors. Imagine the reaction of the Catholic Church if the Magistracy had let this condemned heretic go. What would that say about the purity of the Protestants? From the outset of his exposure to Servetus, William de Trie boasted to his cousin, 'I see vice better conquered here than in all your territories. And although we allow greater liberty in religion and doctrine, we do not suffer the name of God to be blasphemed …. You suffer a heretic, who well deserves to be burned wherever he may be …. And this man is in good repute among you, and is suffered as if he were not wrong. Where I'd like to know is the zeal which you pretend? Where is the police of this fine hierarchy of which you so boast.'[52]

As early as 1532 the Catholics were lamenting Protestant leniency with heretics. For example, Jerome Aleandro (1480– 1542), the papal nuncio who led the opposition to Luther at the Diet of Worms (1521) wrote in April 1532: 'These heretics of Germany, Lutheran or Zwinglian, wherever the Spaniard [Servetus] may be, ought to punish him if they are so very Christian and evangelical and defenders of the faith.'[53] This leniency had been mocked by Catholics when Geneva had banished Anabaptists instead of executing them.[54]

The reformers of Zürich understood this well, writing:

---

52. Ibid., 8:837; quoted in Benjamin Kaplan, *Divided by Faith: Religious Conflict and the Practice of Toleration in Early Modern Europe* (Cambridge, MA: Belknap Press, 2007), 16.

53. Ed. Hugo Laemmer, *Monumenta Vaticana Historiam Ecclesiasticam Saeculi XVI* (Freiburg im Breisgau, 1861), 110, quoted in Bainton, *Hunted Heretic*, 45. Aleandro himself was responsible for the burning of two monks in Antwerp, Netherlands.

54. Naphy, 'Calvin's Geneva,' 32–33.

We think that you ought in this case to manifest much faith and zeal, inasmuch as our churches have abroad the bad reputation of being heretical, and of being particularly favorable to heresy. Holy Providence at this time affords you an opportunity of freeing yourselves and us from that injurious suspicion, if you know how to be vigilant and active in preventing the further spreading of that poison, and we have no doubt but that your Seigneurs will do so.[55]

Heinrich Bullinger, who replaced Ulrich Zwingli as pastor of the Grossmünster in Zürich, hints of this when he writes to Johannes Haller of Bern, 'it was the providence of God that Servetus fled to Geneva so that she might have an opportunity to clear herself of the charge of heresy and blasphemy by punishing him as he deserved.'[56]

Following the execution of Servetus, John Jewel (1522–1571) of England boasted to the Catholics that it was Protestantism that had purged Christianity of Servetus and other like heretics.[57] In the words of François Wendel, 'Tolerance, in the sixteenth century, was not, and could not be, anything but a sign of religious opposition or apathy.'[58] Calvin is thus in the difficult place of currently being condemned by the Catholic Church for participating in the condemnation of Servetus, whereas, in the sixteenth century, the Catholic Church would

---

55. *John Calvin: Tracts and Letters*, 5:435, fn. 2. Upon reading Servetus' *On the Errors of the Trinity*, Philip Melanchthon wrote, 'Good God, what tragedies this question will excite among those who come after us' (*Philippi Melanthonis Opera quae supersunt omnia* [Corpus reformatorum], 2:630, quoted in Bainton, *Hunted Heretic*, 43).

56. *CO*, 14:624.

57. *An Answer to a Certain Book Lately Set Forth by M. Harding, and Entitled, A Confutation of the Apology of the Church of England* (1567), reprinted in *The Works of John Jewel*, edited by John Ayre, 8 volumes (Cambridge: Cambridge University Press, 1848), 3:188.

58. *Calvin: Origins and Development of His Religious Thought* (trans. Philip Mairet; Grand Rapids: Baker, 2002), 98.

have condemned Calvin for participating in the acquittal of Servetus.

The magistrates would not weaken their position in Geneva by appearing impotent before the pastors (who would have the support of the leading reformed Swiss cities), or before the Catholics as tolerating a heretic.[59] It certainly would have looked hypocritical if the city that originally accused Servetus as a heretic (via de Trie), would tolerate his presence. Additionally, the magistrates realized that the Empire could look upon such a rejection of the law as a threat, which could be used as a pretense for war to reclaim the city for Catholicism.

The Swiss Cities Respond to Geneva

By 25 October, the letters returned from the Swiss cities with their verdict on what should be done with Servetus.[60] Essentially serving as a jury for the case, the cities provided a unanimous condemnation of Servetus' doctrine. Although the Swiss cities made no unanimous, official, clear ruling concerning execution, the message of condemnation was clear. In a personal letter from Haller (the minister at Bern) to Bullinger, he writes, 'We explained the primary errors of Servetus point by point to our council at their request. On hearing this they were all so

---

59. Bruce Gordon assesses the situation: 'Calvin could not have Servetus executed. That was the decision of a council not well disposed towards the Frenchman and with which he was locked in battle over excommunication. Servetus provided an opportunity for the magistrates to demonstrate their authority over Calvin, and that is perhaps why his request that the condemned man be put to the sword was rejected. The magistrates understood clearly that harbouring or exonerating a heretic would blacken Geneva's name across Europe. Servetus was a dead man the moment he was recognized in the church service' (*Calvin*, 224).

60. *CO*, 8:808–23, cf. ix, 72ff. for the letters from these cities. Each of these cities had been involved in executing heretics.

indignant that I doubt not they would have burned him had he been detained in their prisons.'[61]

Because of the history of Bern and Geneva, the ruling by Bern's magistrates no doubt made an impact on the magistrates of Geneva. As Calvin writes, 'The Senate of Bern shares this opinion [that Servetus should be treated with severity], and there is a letter from the Senate of Bern that produced no little excitement among us.'[62]

The Execution of Servetus

The magistrates of Geneva made the following judgment on 27 October after they received the letters from the Swiss cities: 'Their Messieurs, having received the opinions of the churches of Basel, Bern, Zürich and Schaffhausen upon the Servetus affair, condemned the said Servetus to be led to Champel and there to be burned alive.'[63] The verdict further reads:

> … desiring to purge the Church of God of such infection and cut off the rotten member, having taken counsel with our citizens and having invoked the name of God to give just judgment … having God and the Holy Scriptures before our eyes, speaking in the name of the Father, Son and Holy Spirit, we now in writing give final sentence and condemn you, Michael Servetus, to be bound and taken to Champel and there attached to a stake and burned with your books to ashes. And so you shall finish your days and give an example to others who would commit the like.[64]

---

61. *CO,* 14:647, quoted in Bainton, *Hunted Heretic,* 137.

62. Ibid., 14:657.

63. *The Register of the Company of Pastors,* 290 (*CO,* 8:830).

64. Ibid., 8:829, quoted in Bainton, *Hunted Heretic,* 141–42.

The sentence was then read to Servetus. Calvin gives his account of Servetus' reaction: 'At times he seemed stunned; then, he would utter sighs which resounded in the whole courtroom; sometimes he screamed like a madman. In short, he had no more composure than a demoniac. Toward the end, his cry became a related roar in Spanish, "Misericordia, misericordia!"'[65]

The justification for this sentence was the accepted law under the Holy Roman Empire, and that of the Code of Justinian that prescribes the death penalty for denial of the Trinity and rebaptism. As mentioned previously, Calvin was unable to vote on the sentence because he was not a citizen of Geneva.

It was at this time that Ami Perrin attempted to prolong the trial by referring it to the Council of Two Hundred, but was overruled.[66]

Realizing that Servetus' execution would take place the following day, Calvin, and only Calvin, made an appeal for a less barbarous form of execution.[67] However, Calvin was denied his request—once again showing that Calvin's opinions and preferences were not the rule in Geneva.[68]

Calvin met with Servetus following the sentencing, and responded to Servetus' plea for pardon:

I protested simply, and it is the truth, that I had never entertained any personal rancor against him. I reminded him gently how I had risked my life more than sixteen years ago to gain him for our Savior. If he would return to reason

---

65. *CO*, 8:498 (Latin), 826 n. 3 (French).

66. 'CCCXXXI–To Farel,' 26 October 1553, in *John Calvin: Tracts and Letters*, 5:436. Bainton concludes, 'It is altogether possible that some of the Libertines out of spite for Calvin sought to release one whom he accused. Yet the party as a whole did not. Claude Rigot, who prosecuted Servetus, was himself a Perrinist, and acted in entire independence of Calvin' (Bainton, *Hunted Heretic*, 122).

67. Ibid., 5:435–36 (cf. *CO*, 14:656–57; 14:590).

68. Ibid., 5:436.

I would faithfully do my best to reconcile him to all good servants of God. And although he had avoided the contest I had never ceased to remonstrate with him kindly in letters. In a word I had used all humanity to the very end, until he being embittered by my good advice hurled all manner of rage and anger against me. I told him that I would pass over everything which concerned me personally. He should rather ask the pardon of God ....[69]

Servetus was condemned and burned at Champel, a hill near the south gate of Geneva on 27 October 1553. Two hours before his execution, Calvin expressed to Servetus, 'I neither hate you nor despise you; nor did I want to be hard in pursuit of you; but I would be as hard as iron when I behold you insulting sound doctrine with so great audacity.'[70] Farel walked with Servetus on the way to the execution site, admonishing him to repent while there was time. There is no credible evidence that Calvin attended the execution or that Servetus' last words were, 'O Jesus, Son of the Eternal God, have pity on me!'[71]

---

69. *CO*, 8:826 (French), 8:460 (Latin), quoted in Bainton, *Hunted Heretic*, 142.

70. Ibid., 8:495.

71. By not praying to the 'Eternal Son,' these often-quoted last words have Servetus holding fast to his doctrine until the very end. This prayer is likely an apocryphal account and is not mentioned by Farel or Beza.

5

FINAL CONSIDERATIONS

An Alternate Ending?

Considering the available evidence, the question must be entertained if Servetus would not have been executed in Geneva if it were not for two key factors: political pressure from Vienne and Servetus' obstinate behavior. Contrary to the view that all anti-Trinitarians were executed in Reformed cities based upon Imperial law, it must be remembered that anti-Trinitarians visited Geneva before and after Servetus without being executed (as was true of Servetus' visits to Basel and Strasbourg). Consequently, it is recognized that the death penalty was not automatically applied in all cases of heresy. Considering that Calvin had ample opportunities to have Servetus arrested and executed prior to his venture to Geneva, and that Calvin spent significant time pleading with Servetus to repent during the trial, a personal vendetta against Servetus by Calvin should also be rejected.

Why then was Servetus executed for anti-Trinitarianism while others in Geneva were not? Firstly, Servetus' prior condemnation in Vienne is significant. Perhaps the primary reason for Servetus' execution is that he had been tried, found guilty, and burned in effigy in Vienne. All of Europe was then watching Geneva to see if this bastion of Protestantism would uphold orthodox theology, or tolerate heresy. Feeling pressure from the Catholics on one hand, and the Genevan pastors with their concern for purity (against Libertarianism) on the other, the magistrates felt compelled to act. The letters from the other Swiss cities confirmed their decision and gave them license to follow through with the execution.

The second factor, which Calvin said was not subordinate to the first,[1] involves Servetus' bizarre behavior during the trial. Even those sympathetic to Servetus recognize the pattern of arrogant, condescending, anti-authoritarian comportment through his life. This was on full display during the trial, and the minutes prove that this type of obstinate heresy was a particular offense to the magistrates.

Calvin's Culpability

A question that is inevitably raised concerning Calvin's involvement is his culpability. For perspective, and to answer those who single out Calvin's support of the death penalty as an abomination, a few other significant reformers will be

---

1. Calvin writes, 'Certainly his arrogance destroyed him not less than his impiety' (*CO*, 9:575. Translation used from Schaff, 578).

examined.[2] Theodore Beza (1519–1605), the successor of Calvin in Geneva, writes:

> Servetus was justly punished at Geneva, not as a sectary, but as a monster, made up of nothing but impiety and horrid blasphemies, with which, by his speeches and writings, for the space of thirty years, he had infected both heaven and earth. Even now it is impossible to state how much he has increased the rage of Satan, since the flame, raised by him, first seized upon Poland then Transylvania and Hungary, and would to God it had not extended even farther.[3]

Bullinger (pastor in Zürich following the death of Zwingli) also writes to Beza, 'But what is your most honorable senate of Geneva going to do with that blasphemous wretch Servetus? If they are wise, and do their duty, they will put him to death, that all the world may perceive that Geneva desires the glory of Christ to be maintained inviolate.'[4]

Largely known as an irenic spirit, Philip Melanchthon helped to make Luther more palatable, even largely being responsible for the conciliatory Augsburg Confession of 1530.[5]

---

2. Jules Bonnet comments, 'The error of Calvin in the death of Servetus was, we may say, altogether that of his age, inasmuch as men of the most conciliating and moderate dispositions, viz., Bucer, Œcolampadius, Melanchthon, and Bullinger, were as one in their approval of the condemnation of the unfortunate Spanish innovator. One may deeply deplore this error without insulting the Reformation, and combine in a just measure that pity which a great victim demands, with respect for those men whom an unhappy time made the accusers and the judges of Servetus' (*John Calvin: Tracts and Letters*, 5:436, fn. 2).

3. *The Life of John Calvin*, translated by Francis Sibson (Philadelphia: J. Whetham, 1836), 60.

4. 'Letter CCCL,' *Original Letters Relative to the English Reformation* (Cambridge: Cambridge University Press, 1846), 2:742.

5. Calvin's letter to Melanchthon on 18 June 1550 illustrates Calvin's frustration with Melanchthon's lack of resolve to maintain true doctrine. Calvin admonished him, 'strive the more manfully' in 'unflinching

In response to Calvin's publication of *Defense of the Orthodox Faith Against the Monstrous Errors of the Spaniard Michael Servetus*, Melanchthon writes, 'I have read your answer to the blasphemies of Servetus and approve of your piety and opinions. I judge also that the Genevan Senate acted correctly to put an end to this obstinate man, who could never cease blaspheming. And I wonder at those who disapprove of this severity.'[6] Not only does this statement support capital punishment for heresy, but identifies the Genevan Senate as the authority to exact the punishment.

The testimony of the amiable peacemaker of the Reformation, Martin Bucer of Strasbourg, is more graphic than that of Melanchthon. Despite Bucer's shepherding of Calvin through difficult days, and even warning Calvin about Farel's fiery influence upon his temperament, Calvin describes Bucer's sentiments years prior to Servetus' execution: 'It was [Servetus] whom that faithful minister of Christ, Master Bucer of holy memory, in other respects of a mild disposition, declared from the pulpit to be worthy of having his bowels pulled out, and torn to pieces.'[7]

Peter Martyr Vermigli (1499–1562), a reformed leader from Italy writes:

> As regards the Spaniard Servetus, I do not have anything else to say except that he was a genuine son of the devil, whose plague-bearing and hateful teaching has been spread about everywhere. The magistrates who exacted from him the

---

steadfastness.' Calvin even acknowledged to Melanchthon, 'I know how much you are horrified at the charge of rude severity' ('CCLXIII–To Melanchthon,' 18 June 1550, in *John Calvin: Tracts and Letters*, 5:270–75).

6. 'Melanchthon to Calvin', 14 October 1554 in *CO*, 15:268, quoted in Gordon, 224.

7. 'CCCXXVII–To Sulzer,' 8 September 1553, in *John Calvin: Tracts and Letters*, 5:428.

supreme penalty should not be accused since they could get from him no indications of amendment and his blasphemies were utterly intolerable.[8]

The great reformer of Scotland, John Knox (1514–1572) went so far as to write against Anabaptist detractors in *The Execution of Servetus for Blasphemy, Heresy, and Obstinate Anabaptism, Defended*.[9] He writes:

> Ye will not easily admit that Servetus was convicted of blasphemy; for if so be, ye must be compelled to confess (except that ye will refuse God) that the sentence of death executed against him was not cruelty; neither yet that the judges who justly pronounced that sentence were murderers nor persecutors; but that this death was the execution of God's judgment, and they the true and faithful servants of God, who, when no other remedy was found, did take away iniquity from amongst them. That God hath appointed death by his law, without mercy, to be executed upon the blasphemers, is evident by that which is written, Leviticus 24.[10]

Moving on in history, the great English Puritan John Owen (1616–1683) writes, 'To this height of atheism and blasphemy had Satan wrought up the spirit of the man [Servetus]; so that I must say he is the only person in the world, that I ever read or heard of, that ever died upon the account of religion, in

8. *Life, Letters and Sermons: Peter Martyr Vermigli*, edited and translated by John Patrick Donnelly. Peter Martyr Library (Kirksville: Thomas Jefferson State University Press, 1999), 4:154. Quoted in Jason Zuidema, *Peter Martyr Vermigli (1499–1562) and the Outward Instruments of Divine Grace* (Göttingen: Vandenhoeck & Ruprecht, 2015), 74.

9. In *The Reformation's Light*, edited by C. Matthew McMahon and Therese McMahon (Coconut Beach, FL: A Puritan's Mind and Puritan Publications), 195–207.

10. Ibid., 199.

reference to whom the zeal of them that put him to death may be acquitted. But of these things God will judge.'[11]

Scottish Presbyterian Samuel Rutherford (1600–1661) also comments on Servetus: 'It was justice, not cruelty, yea mercy to the Church of God, to take away the life of Servetus, who used such spiritual and diabolic cruelty to many thousand souls, whom he did pervert, and by his Book, does yet lead into perdition.'[12]

Finally, scholastic theologian Francis Turretin (1623–1687), famous for his *Institutes of Elenctic Theology* writes, 'They who traduce the punishment inflicted upon the most impure Servetus as unjust and cruel, that from it they may excite hatred against the distinguished magistracy of Geneva and especially against that great man of God, Calvin, have never sufficiently weighed the atrocity of the crime.'[13]

---

11. *The Works of John Owen*, edited by Thomas Russell, 16 volumes (London: R. Baynes, 1826), 8:lxii.

12. *A Free Disputation Against Pretended Liberty of Conscience* (London: Printed by R.I. for Andrew Crook, 1649), 290.

13. *Institutes of Elenctic Theology*, 3 volumes (Phillipsburg, NJ: P&R, 1992), 3:335.

CONCLUSION

Doctrinal proclivities have marred the way authors have written about the execution of Servetus. In some circles, arguments against intolerant Calvinism have calcified the idea that Calvin was the prosecutor, judge, jury and executioner for Servetus.[1] The evidence has shown this not to be the case.

On the other hand, some supporters of Calvin have ignored or whitewashed evidence that would shed a negative light on Calvin. For example, following the release of a tract critical of

---

1. Derek W.H. Thomas responds, 'His execution is not an example of intolerant Calvinism, but of a layer of sixteenth-century civil jurisprudence in central Europe, where various lifestyles were considered untenable and punishable by law in a way that humanist societies of our own day would react to with apoplexy' ('Who was John Calvin?', edited by Burk Parsons in *John Calvin: A Heart for Devotion, Doctrine & Doxology* [Lake Mary, FL: Reformation Trust, 2008], 24).

Servetus' execution (*Historia de morte Serveti*), Calvin continued to passionately support the magistrates' actions against Servetus in his notoriously impulsive and uncharacteristically unorganized *Defensio orthodoxae fidei de sacra Trinitate, contra prodigiosos errores Michaelis Serveti Hispani* ... (1554).[2] This attitude continued in his correspondences and treatises, despite growing criticism.[3] Even nine years after the execution, Calvin wrote:

> Servetus suffered the penalty due to his heresies, but was it by my will? Certainly his arrogance destroyed him not less than his impiety. And what crime was it of mine if our Council, at my exhortation, indeed, but in conformity with the opinion of several Churches, took vengeance on his execrable blasphemies? Let Baudouin abuse me as long as he will,

2. Calvin writes, 'Whoever shall now contend that it is unjust to put heretics and blasphemers to death will knowingly and willingly incur their very guilt. This is not laid down on human authority; it is God who speaks and prescribes a perpetual rule for his Church. It is not in vain that he banishes all those human affections which soften our hearts; that he commands paternal love and all the benevolent feelings between brothers, relations, and friends to cease; in a word, that he almost deprives men of their nature in order that nothing may hinder their holy zeal. Why is so implacable a severity exacted but that we may know that God is defrauded of his honor, unless the piety that is due to him be preferred to all human duties, and that when his glory is to be asserted, humanity must be almost obliterated from our memories' (*CO*, 8:xxix–xxxiii, quoted in Schaff, *History of the Christian Church*, 8:791–92).

3. This debate continued over the next two years with works such as *De Haereticis, an sint persequendi* (Martinus Bellius/ Sébastien Castellion), *De Haereticis a civili magistratu puniendis* (Beza), *De haereticis non puniendis* (Castellion), and *Contra libellum Calvini* (Castellion). At the end of his life, Calvin wrote, 'Such monsters should be smothered, as I have done here, by the execution of Michel Servetus the Spaniard. Do not imagine that in [sic] future any one will take it into his head to do the like' ('XVII–To Monseigneur, Monseigneur du Poet, Grand Chamberlain of Navarre and Governor of the Town of Montelimart, at Crest,' 8 September 1561, in *John Calvin: Tracts and Letters*, 7:440).

provided that, by the judgment of Melanchthon, posterity owes me a debt of gratitude for having purged the Church of so pernicious a monster.[4]

What are Christians to make of Calvin's attitude towards Servetus? Taking into account the overwhelming evidence that execution for heresy was acceptable at the time (it was Imperial law), that it was practiced among the major Protestant cities, and that the killing of Servetus was approved of by major Protestant theologians, it should give serious pause to anyone who would single out Calvin for condemnation.

In fact, Ronald S. Wallace writes, 'There was no place in the world of the day either Protestant or Catholic where Servetus would have met with anything but a sentence of death.'[5] Alister McGrath concurs:

> To target him [Calvin] in this way—when the manner of his involvement was, to say the least, oblique—and overlook the much greater claims to infamy of other individuals and institutions raises difficult questions concerning the precommitments of his critics. Servetus was the *only* individual put to death for his religious opinions in Geneva during Calvin's lifetime, at a time when executions of this nature were commonplace elsewhere.[6]

Despite this evidence, Calvin's approval of the execution cannot be ignored or minimized. Is it sufficient to say that Calvin was simply a child of his age, or as the leading Protestant theologian

---

4. *CO,* 9:575. Translation used from Schaff, 578.
5. *Calvin, Geneva and the Reformation* (Eugene, OR: Wipf & Stock, 1998), 80.
6. *A Life of John Calvin,* 116. It should be remembered that Gentile was condemned to death in Geneva for heresy in 1557, which was rescinded following his recantation.

of the day, should he have known better?[7] The same principle can be used of other significant figures in Church history, such as Jonathan Edwards (1703–1758), who owned slaves.

Modern sensitivities may lead to a knee-jerk reaction that claims slavery and capital punishment for blasphemy should always be condemned, regardless of the time period. By being intolerant of the sixteenth century ethic, there is a danger of becoming intolerant twenty-first century Christians. G.K. Chesterton warns against this attitude: 'It is not bigotry to be certain that we are right; but it is bigotry to be *unable to imagine* how we might possibly have gone wrong.'[8]

A significant challenge to this anachronistic thinking is to consider that both slavery and execution for blasphemy are described and regulated in Scripture, but not condemned. If execution and slavery must always be denounced, what does that say about the ultimate Author of the Bible?

How can this tension be resolved? Even in Scripture, redemptive movement toward a higher ethic is observed from the Old Testament to the New Testament. History cannot be viewed in a vacuum, so it is natural for God to work in culture, and not apart from it. As a result, God did not outlaw slavery, but regulated it.

Following the trajectory of ethics through the Bible and into the New Covenant era, it is expected that the Holy Spirit will continue to guide the Church into truth which is based upon the authoritative principles found in Scripture. This is why we

---

7.   Today there is a monument standing at the site where Servetus was burned, it reads: 'Dutiful and grateful followers of Calvin our great Reformer, yet condemning an error which was that of his age, and strongly attached to liberty of conscience, according to the true principles of the Reformation and of the Gospel, we have erected this expiatory monument. October 27th, 1903.'

8.   *The Catholic Church and Conversion* (New York: Macmillan, 1950), 27.

see movement regarding women's rights, the abolition of slavery, capital punishment reform, rejection of polygamy, and so on. If toleration can be extended to the biblical Author for working within a culture with an ethic that many find unpalatable in the twenty-first century, how can the same courtesy not be granted to the sixteenth century?

Since the writing of history is an ethical responsibility, it is important to be cautious of anachronism.[9] To judge another culture and time based upon one's own is unfair, and is a violation of the golden rule to treat others as one wants to be treated. As such, anachronistic judgments are unethical. Each time period must be judged by the prevailing laws of the time, not those of the future.[10] Primary evidence of this, as previously mentioned, is Scripture itself. Charity is thus needed to evaluate those with whom we agree theologically, and those with whom we do not.

In chronological snobbery it is very easy to see the sins of our fathers—to expose them, to embarrass them, and to prop ourselves up as being intellectually and morally advanced.

---

9. See Carl R. Trueman, *Histories and Fallacies* (Wheaton, IL: Crossway, 2010).

10. Paul Henry writes: 'It is here that Calvin appears in his real character; and a nearer consideration of the proceeding, —examined, that is, from the point of view furnished by the age in which it took place, —will completely exonerate him from blame. His conduct was not determined by personal feeling: it was the consequence of a struggle which this great man had carried on for years against tendencies to a corruption of doctrine which threatened the church with ruin. Every age must be judged according to its prevailing laws; and Calvin cannot be fairly accused of any greater offense than that with which we may be charged for punishing certain crimes with death. It has been rightly said, that both the legal and theological feeling of the age, expressed as we find it in a variety of striking forms, allows not a shadow of suspicion to fall upon Calvin's integrity for demanding a judgment which was, in every respect, justified by the laws of the state' (*The Life and Times of John Calvin, the Great Reformer*, vol. 2, translated by Henry Stebbing [London: Whittaker and Company, 1849], 160).

While it would be a disservice to our fathers not to learn from their failures, this must be done tactfully, with respect, and as if they were looking over our shoulders as we are writing about them. Appreciate them, learn from them, honor them.

Regardless of how these questions are answered, a valuable inquiry is: 'How would our predecessors want us to learn from their failures?' Primarily, they would affirm that they are not the ultimate arbiters of truth. Luther and Calvin both attest to this. The same principle could be applied to any figure in Scripture, save Jesus Christ. None were sinless and all have records of failure. This applies to Adam, Abraham, David, Solomon, Hezekiah, John, Paul, et al.[11]

Could God have hidden the faults of our forebearers? Yes, and there is a reason why He did not. In God's design, humanity's sin points us to the perfect One, the Lord Jesus Christ. We are to worship no man except Him. As Schaff writes, 'History knows only of one spotless being—the Saviour of sinners. Human greatness and purity are spotted by marks of infirmity, which forbid idolatry. Large bodies cast large shadows, and great virtues are often coupled with great vices.'[12]

These figures of the past serve as tutors to learn from in our own walk (Rom. 15:4; 1 Cor. 10:11; Heb. 13:7). In the case of Calvin, perhaps he would have us learn from his failures to be more forbearing when wronged, teachable, gracious in speech, open to correction (even from enemies), compassionate with the lost, and willing to reevaluate traditions and potential blind-spots when there is growing criticism. In the theological realm,

---

11. As a result, we should have caution in entertaining the question of rejecting a man's doctrine because of transgression. David's sin with Bathsheba not only included adultery, but lying, debauchery (Uriah had more wisdom drunk than David did sober), and murder, and yet, consider the significant portion of Scripture that is about or by him. You are in this company, so be thankful that God uses you!

12. Schaff, 8:687.

it is helpful to think through the theological ramifications of one's understanding of the identity of Israel and the Church, and Law and grace, all of which contribute to the limitation or control of the Church in political affairs.

While the debate will continue concerning Christians in history and the extent of their ethical responsibility to fight such things as slavery and execution for heresy, Christians should agree that charity should be maintained when examining the shortcomings of our fathers, which are only seen because we stand upon the vantage point of their achievements.[13]

---

13. As Peter of Blois [twelfth century] writes, 'However dogs may bark at me, and pigs grunt, I shall always imitate the writings of the ancients; these shall be my study, nor, while my strength lasts, shall the sun find me idle. We are like dwarfs on the shoulders of giants, by whose grace we see farther than they. Our study of the works of the ancients enables us to give fresh life to their finer ideas, and rescue them from time's oblivion and man's neglect' ('Epistola XCII: Ad Reginaldum Bathoniens. Episcopum' in *Patrologia Latina*, edited by J.P. Migne, 217 volumes [Paris: 1844–1864], 207:290).

APPENDIX: SUMMARY

1. Imperial law stated that Anabaptism and denying the Trinity were heresies punishable by death.

2. Execution for heresy was supported and practiced by Protestants (Lutherans, Reformed, Anglicans, Anabaptist factions, and Protestant confessions), Catholics, and Orthodox.

3. With most theologians of his time, Calvin supported the death penalty for unrepentant heresy.

4. Since Servetus broke Imperial law with his doctrine, his execution was lawful and anticipated by himself years prior to the event.

5. Servetus taught his doctrine in Basel and Strasbourg, and was expelled, not executed (although he was arrested in Basel during his second visit and was released as a result of

his recantation). Hence, Imperial law was not universally followed.

6. At a time when Protestants were being burned alive for their faith, Calvin risked his life by being willing to publicly meet Servetus in Paris in order to convince him of his error, but Servetus did not keep the appointment.

7. Servetus was arrested by Catholics in Vienne and sentenced to death by burning. Although Servetus escaped before the sentence could be carried out, he was burned in effigy, *in absentia*.

8. Following heated correspondence with Servetus, Calvin wrote a letter to a friend, which threatened Servetus with death if he came to Geneva. The same day he wrote another letter expressing the joy he would have if God worked repentance in Servetus. These letters are to be interpreted by understanding the extent of Calvin's authority in Geneva.

9. Although Calvin knew Servetus' true identity, he did not pursue his arrest by reporting him to the authorities, nor did he entice him to Geneva to entrap him.

10. Calvin was hesitant to send incriminating evidence to the Catholics trying Servetus, preferring to fight heretics with doctrine.

11. Knowing of Servetus' ongoing trial for breaking Imperial law and his obstinacy in his heresy, Calvin ordered Servetus' arrest following his identification in Geneva.

12. Upon Servetus' arrest, Calvin supported the death penalty, although he claims not to mention the form of punishment at the trial.

13. Calvin was not a resident of Geneva during the Servetus trial, and had no authority to vote or hold office.

14. The magistrates of Geneva were largely opposed to Calvin's ministry during the trial of Servetus. Barring his expulsion from Geneva in 1538, Calvin never had such minimal authority as he did during Servetus' trial. This is made evident by his offers to resign during the trial, in his conviction that he would be fired from his pastorate during this time, and in his farewell sermon.

15. The magistrates assigned Calvin to outline charges against Servetus, but he was neither judge, nor prosecutor, nor on a jury.

16. The Swiss cities of Basel, Bern, Zurich and Schaffhausen agreed that the threat of Servetus should be eliminated.

17. Considering that anti-Trinitarians were present in Geneva before and after Servetus, but were not killed, the deciding facts behind Servetus' execution are: Servetus was condemned and burned in effigy in Vienne; Catholics pressured Geneva to extradite Servetus; other Reformed cities ruled that Servetus was guilty; there was an awareness that the purity of Protestantism was being tested; and there were arguments that the Imperial army would have grounds for attacking the city if Geneva did not uphold Imperial law.

18. Servetus' conduct during the trial (and through his life) has caused some to question his sanity. He demanded that Calvin be exterminated and that all of Calvin's property be given to himself. Servetus' attacks against the magistrates and the pastors are thought to be another strong reason why he was executed. Considering Servetus is largely thought of as a champion of toleration and freedom of conscience, it is helpful to note that he supported execution for obstinate heresy, that he believed in the exclusivity of

His view of God, and that all tyrants of the Church should be destroyed.

19. Calvin requested a more humane method of execution, but was rejected by the magistrates.

20. Servetus was burned alive, but in the absence of Calvin.

21. Following attacks on the execution of Servetus, Calvin wrote, *Defense of the Orthodox Faith against the Monstrous Errors of the Spaniard Michael Servetus*. In this work, and subsequent letters, Calvin defends Servetus' execution by the magistrates and indicates satisfaction concerning his involvement in Servetus' condemnation. This doubling down and insensitivity by Calvin is justifiably criticized by Calvin's supporters.

22. Prominent Protestant leaders of the time such as Bucer, Bullinger, Beza, Knox, Peter Martyr Vermigli, and Melanchthon all agreed that Servetus was rightly executed. Considering that other Reformation luminaries such as Zwingli, Cranmer, and Queen Elizabeth I were directly involved in executions for heresy, it is problematic to indict Calvin for his involvement in Servetus' execution while ignoring the activity of his fellow reformers.